Crosscurrents / MODERN CRITIQUES

Harry T. Moore, *General Editor*

In a Minor Chord

*Three Afro-American Writers
and Their Search for Identity*

Darwin T. Turner

WITH A PREFACE BY
Harry T. Moore

SOUTHERN ILLINOIS UNIVERSITY PRESS
Carbondale and Edwardsville

FEFFER & SIMONS, INC.
London and Amsterdam

Contents

Preface

Darwin Turner's brief but vital and thought-crammed Introduction to his study of three Afro-American authors, which follows this preface, deals with the difficulties of black writers not only among whites but among their own people: the latter often criticize such authors either for writing about the wrong kind of blacks, or for writing about blacks in the wrong way, or for being Uncle Toms. This situation is not really unnatural, given the confused conditions of our culture, and with the help of vigorously dedicated men and women of all shades of color we may one day—and soon, too—come to a fuller understanding of the realities involved, and so we may find a way of correcting various errors.

The black-and-white "dialogue" which has gone on so intensely for several years now may in a little while do much to help many of our social and literary misunderstandings and oppositions. One of the good things which has emerged from the recent "dialogue" is the upgrading of various Afro-American writers by white readers.

Professor Turner in his Introduction refers to the awarding of various prizes to recent Afro-American writers, but the acceptance of black authors has gone beyond that. Colleges have courses in black literature, and anthologies of black poets thrive, hardbound and paperback. Perspectives are being adjusted.

It wasn't like this in "the old times." Then, the offi-

cial college anthologies of writers contained white authors almost entirely, once in a while including the work
of the well-treated eighteenth-century slave, Phillis
Wheatley, but including it for quaintness rather than
quality. I have at hand an American Literature anthology
left over from undergraduate days, The Literature of
America, by Quinn, Baugh, and Howe, published in
1929; it doesn't include Phillis Wheatley, but it does
have Paul Laurence Dunbar, who died in 1906. He is
represented by three poems, although a Thomas S. Jones,
Jr., has six. Who in the world was he? He doesn't appear
in the fifth edition of The Oxford Companion to Literature (1965). And Brian Hooker, whom some of us
remember only as the translator of Cyrano de Bergerac
for Walter Hampden, has three poems in the book;
Joyce Kilmer has four; much space is taken up with
stories by Booth Tarkington, Anne Douglas Sedgwick,
Margaret Deland, and others—imagine their work being
read in universities! The anthology of course provides
nothing by Langston Hughes, who by 1929 had published two volumes, including The Weary Blues (1926);
and where is Charles Waddell Chesnutt?

A critical study, Recent American Poets: From the
Puritans to the Present (1968), by Hyatt H. Waggoner,
is in the main an excellent book and an extensive one,
but there is not even passing reference to Dunbar,
Hughes, Countee Cullen, or various other black poets.
The 1947 edition of The Literature of the United States,
by Blair, Hornberger, and Stewart, in all the fullness of
its two big volumes, didn't admit a single black author,
though later editions eventually did so; the February 1,
1971 issue of Publishers' Weekly carried a letter from
the National Council of Teachers of English's Task
Force on Racism and Bias in the Teaching of English,
congratulating the editors of the 1969 edition for including Afro-American writers who had not appeared in

the 1966 edition. And just now a new anthology has come in the mail, the three volumes of the fifth edition of American Poetry and Prose, edited by Norman Foerster and others. This contains three poems by Phillis Wheatley and, although admitting that her verse was imitative (of Alexander Pope and others), it also states that this "work has been underrated and overpraised" and refers the reader to her Poems (1966), edited by Julian D. Mason, Jr., and White Over Black: American Attitudes Toward the Negro, 1550–1812 (1968), by Winthrop D. Jordan. Interestingly enough, the first Foerster volume also includes a tribute to Phillis Wheatley by another educated slave, Jupiter Hammon. Chesnutt appears in the second volume, and so does Frederick Douglass. In the third, we find not only Hughes but also Jean Toomer and Claude McKay, as well as two living Afro-American writers, Ralph Ellison and Robert Hayden. It's a new world we're in.

Darwin Turner's book is an important contribution to a fuller comprehension of that world. Darwin Turner, a graduate of the University of Cincinnati and a Ph.D. from Chicago, was for several years Dean of the North Carolina Agricultural and Technical College and is now Professor of English at the University of Michigan. He has written on Nathaniel Hawthorne and on various Afro-American writers. In the present book he discusses three black authors, all dead now, whom he is helping to rescue from semioblivion. I can recall, in undergraduate days, reading about one of them, Jean Toomer (1894–1967), in Paul Rosenfeld's illuminating book of criticism, Men Seen (1925), which contained generous quotations from Toomer; and while I was still an undergraduate, at the University of Chicago, I had the pleasure of meeting him; a man with a look of distinction. The friend who introduced us was an Adlerian psychoanalyst; Dr. Turner mentions that Toomer later underwent Jungian analysis. In literature he then seemed a minor figure, despite the high praise of his work in the preceding decade, but just now—thanks partly to Darwin Turner and our mutual friend Arna Bontemps—Toomer has become an important minor figure. In the present volume, Darwin Turner traces his career, showing the difficulties he encountered even after turning out work that earned the praise not only of Rosenfeld but also of Waldo Frank and Sherwood Anderson. Darwin Turner's essay on Toomer is done "in depth," with sympathetic analysis.

Professor Turner brings equal gifts of understanding to his discussion of Countee Cullen (1903–46) "the lost Ariel" and "the poet laureate of the Harlem Renaissance." Yet, as Dr. Turner shows, Cullen never lived up to his early promise. He wound up writing children's books. The final collection of his poems, however, On These I Stand, which he put together shortly before his death, contains excellent work. Cullen had known well the difficulties of being a black man, and sometimes he resolved his troubles by compromise, sometimes by facing them. This study of him and his work is extremely valuable in the large sense as well as in particulars.

Zora Neale Hurston (1903–60) is a black author who, as Dr. Turner sees her, "remained a wandering minstrel." According to her own account, she had less difficulty, at least in early life, in the white world than other Afro-American writers. In an autobiographical statement in the 1940s she said, "I have never been able to achieve race prejudice. I just see people. I see the man first, and his race as just another detail of his description." As Professor Turner notes, "It was eccentric but perhaps appropriate for her to take a job as a cook and maid for a white family and to die in poverty."

Before that time, however, Miss Hurston had written some notable stories and novels, beginning with her third book, Their Eyes Were Watching God. Through-out, Dr. Turner deals with her work both ideationally and technically, acutely measuring her failures and successes, always suggesting why she is an author for Americans to read, even though, like Toomer and Cullen, she didn't fully realize her potential and must be regarded as being "in a minor chord." But we should remember that a minor chord can sound tonal depths.

I think that, in the midst of the new estimates of Afro-American writers, Darwin Turner's book will be a landmark. He is a commentator who sees all sides of perplexing questions, one who can both analyze and explain and can do so illuminatingly.

HARRY T. MOORE

Southern Illinois University
February 12, 1971

Acknowledgments

I would like to make the following acknowledgments for permission to quote from previously published material and personal letters:

Quotations from the letters of Sherwood Anderson to Jean Toomer are reprinted by permission of Harold Ober Associates Incorporated.

Poetry excerpts from *The Black Christ and Other Poems* and *Color*, by Countee Cullen, are reprinted with the permission of Harper and Row, Publishers.

Quotations from the book *Dust Tracks on a Road* by Zora Neale Hurston. Copyright, 1942, by Zora Neale Hurston. Renewal, ©, 1970 by John C. Hurston. Reprinted by permission of J. B. Lippincott Company. Quotations from the book *Jonah's Gourd Vine* by Zora Neale Hurston. Copyright, 1934, by Zora Neale Hurston. Reprinted by permission of J. B. Lippincott.

Quotations from *Cane* by Jean Toomer. Copyright © 1951 by Jean Toomer. Reprinted with permission of Liveright Publishing Corp., New York.

Part of Chapter 1 was originally published in the January 1969 issue of *Negro Digest* as "Jean Toomer's *Cane*" by Darwin T. Turner. Copyright © 1969 by *Negro Digest*. It is reprinted, with revisions, by permission of *Black World*.

I wish to express appreciation to Mrs. Marjorie Content Toomer for permission to quote from the unpublished letters and papers of Jean Toomer, and to Mrs. Jean Frank and Mrs. Elizabeth D. Munson for permission to quote from their husbands' letters to Toomer.

I am also indebted to Professor Arna Bontemps, who encouraged my desire to pursue further research in Jean Toomer, and who, in the position he held as Director of the Library at Fisk University, provided me with access to the Toomer manuscripts upon which the study of Toomer is based. I am also grateful to Professor O. B. Hardison, Director of the Folger Library, who immeasurably assisted my efforts to continue my research; the American Council of Learned Societies, which provided a grant-in-aid enabling me to undertake the research in Toomer; and the North Carolina-Duke Universities Cooperative Program in the Humanities, which provided a fellowship enabling me to continue research in the works of Countee Cullen, Zora Neale Hurston, and other Afro-American writers. A special word of appreciation is due President Lewis C. Dowdy of North Carolina Agricultural and Technical State University, who made it possible for me to accept the fellowship and who, in numerous ways, furnished assistance that facilitated my completing and publishing my research.

I wish also to thank Mrs. Fannie Garrison and Miss Bonnie Floyd, who helped prepare the final copy, and the librarians at Fisk University and the University of North Carolina at Chapel Hill, who helped me gather materials.

Above all, I want to express my gratitude to my wife Jeanne, whose thoughtfulness and encouragement revived and sustained me at critical stages of the research and the writing.

Introduction

The Harlem Renaissance of the 1920s was the most exciting and important cultural movement which Afro-Americans had ever experienced. In fact, it was the first period during which a significant number of Americans actually examined Afro-American culture closely and encouraged increased productivity for artistic reasons.

By 1920, Afro-Americans had been publishing literary works for more than one hundred and fifty years: Lucy Terry, a slave in Deerfield, Massachusetts, is known to have composed a poem as early as 1746; Brutus and Jupiter Hammon wrote poetry and essays in the 1760s; and Phillis Wheatley, born in Africa and enslaved in Boston, had a collection of poems published in 1773. In the first half of the nineteenth century, while America debated the issue of slavery with intensifying fervor, additional Afro-Americans earned modest reputations in literature—in particular, William Wells Brown for fiction and essays, Frances Harper for poetry, and Frederick Douglass for nonfiction. Nevertheless, during the first half of the century Americans generally turned to black writers for pathetic recitations of the agonies of slavery rather than for artistic literature.

After the Civil War, collections of spirituals and Joel Chandler Harris's collections of folktales familiarized some Americans with Afro-American talent for song and tale. Others, however, continued to doubt the educability and the artistic creativity of Afro-Americans. The first sponsors of Paul Laurence Dunbar rejoiced to discover his poetic talent, not so much because they considered it a possible source for significant contributions to American literature, but because it gave them opportunity to demonstrate the creative potential of a black American. Even the respected critic William Dean Howells, who praised Dunbar enthusiastically in 1896, revealed ignorance of black writers, an ignorance which persuaded Howells and other critics to underestimate the literary potential of Africa's descendants. In the *Atlantic Monthly* in 1896, Howells praised Dunbar as the first individual of African ancestry to show innate literary talent; when reminded, or informed, that the very popular French writer, Alexandre Dumas, was of African descent, Howells modified his statement to describe Dunbar as the first Afro-American to show innate talent for literature. Howells did not know or had forgotten the African ancestry of Alexander Pushkin, one of the greatest of all Russian authors; and in 1896 he apparently knew nothing about the Afro-American Charles W. Chesnutt, who had published his first short story in the *Atlantic Monthly* more than ten years before Howells became acquainted with Dunbar's work.

A few talented writers earned national attention at the end of the nineteenth century and in the first years of the twentieth. Dunbar became one of America's most popular poets. The less popular Charles Chesnutt evoked critics' respect as a writer of fiction, and W. E. B. DuBois delighted academicians with his scholarly historical and sociological studies and his brilliant essays. Nevertheless, America, in general, continued to judge such writers as exceptions rather than as examples of the creative potential of Afro-Americans.

Ironically, interest in and respect for Afro-American culture developed to a peak during the same decade in which the Ku Klux Klan revived its membership and organized klans farther north than ever before. Ironically, also, this decade of the twenties followed one in which few publishers, editors, or producers permitted Afro-Americans opportunity to demonstrate their talent.

The change in attitude may be attributed to events and ideas which coincided during World War I. One, during the Jazz Age, as the decade is popularly remembered, Americans developed respect for the music—especially the jazz and the blues of black Americans. Performers and listeners alike learned to seek out such black jazz artists as the aging King Oliver or the young and exciting Louis Armstrong and Duke Ellington, who were forming their first bands. The interest in music may have stimulated a desire to learn more about other creative endeavors of Afro-Americans.

Two, rebelling against the mores of what seemed to be a conservative society, many young white Americans saw in black people the models for the kind of freedom they wanted. Not knowing the Harlemite who worked from 8 A.M. to 6 P.M., but inferring racial character from the free improvisations of jazz, many whites imposed on Afro-Americans the image of an amoral, unrepressed individual, happy because he was not burdened by the inhibitions of civilized white society.

Still other Americans, inspired by the democratic slogans preached during "the war to end all wars," may have considered it their humanitarian responsibility to examine more closely the American citizens who had not reaped the full benefits of democracy. Furthermore, white artists—not merely musicians but also writers—became interested in black Americans, although primarily as representatives of a primitive culture. In 1917, Ridgely Torrence wrote *Three Plays for a Negro Theater*. Three years later Eugene O'Neill produced *The Emperor Jones*, in which he dramatized the thesis that savagery lurks beneath the civilized veneer of the Afro-American. Within ten years, these writers were followed by Mary Wiborg (*Taboo*), Em Jo Basshe (*Earth*), DuBose Heyward (*Porgy*), Waldo Frank (*Holiday*), Sherwood Anderson (*Dark Laughter*), Paul Green (with numerous plays), Julia Peterkin (*Black April*), Carl van Vechten (*Nigger Heaven*), William Faulkner (*The Sound and the Fury*), and Marc Connelly (*Green Pastures*), to name only some of the better known.

Undoubtedly, blacks themselves helped to win respect for their culture. Such Afro-American scholars as Carter G. Woodson and Benjamin Brawley searched for achievements which they could praise and publicize. Alain Locke, a professor of philosophy at Howard University in Washington, and Charles S. Johnson, editor of *Opportunity* magazine, joined white Carl van Vechten in a search for black talent. Experiences in Europe had developed among black soldiers a pride in themselves and their race. Availability of jobs had encouraged blacks to migrate north to a dignity and a freedom which, though limited, were greater than they had experienced previously.

No matter what the cause or causes, the fact is that during the 1920s white Americans became interested in the culture of Afro-Americans, and the blacks gave them something to see. It was the decade of the "Harlem Renaissance," so-called because many of the young, productive artists migrated to Harlem; or it was the decade of the "Negro Renaissance," or, simply, the era of the "New Negro." And writers abounded. Claude McKay, a West Indian, demonstrated versatility in poetry and fiction in re-creating the tender and the bitter moods of the New Negro. Wallace Thurman and George Schuyler wrote brilliant satires. Rudolph Fisher mixed satire and realism into faithful depictions of Harlem, and Jessie Fauset tried to depict the aspects of Negro life not continually affected by interracial conflicts. Young Langston Hughes earned respect for happy and loving poems and stories about Northern blacks, and his friend Arna Bontemps sympathetically revealed Southern blacks. James Weldon Johnson not only wrote poetry himself but even edited an anthology of Afro-American poetry. Alain Locke edited *The New Negro* (1925), an anthology of criticism and creativity, *Four Negro Poets* (1927), and *Plays of Negro Life* (1927).

It was truly an era of Afro-American artistic exuberance exemplified by black writers who sentimentally or realistically reproduced black primitives; who satirized their black social, economic, and intellectual peers; who laughed at themselves and their white neighbors; who searched for their heritage; and who found pride in themselves and their ancestors. *The writers and their works sang a paean to blackness, written in a major key. But a melancholy minor chord was sounded by a triad*—Jean Toomer, generally acknowledged to be the most artistic black craftsman of those who wrote before 1950; Countee Cullen, the precocious poet laureate of the Renaissance; and Zora Neale Hurston, the most competent black female novelist before 1950.

At first glance, one might assume that these three patterned after their contemporaries. They wrote about primitives; they satirized their peers; and they searched for their heritage. But they found scant satisfaction in their search. Upon closer examination, they seem to be wanderers—talented artists, perhaps the most talented Afro-American writers of the decade, who searched in creativity and in life for some intangible satisfaction which they failed to find.

The purpose of this study is to examine the lives and particularly the works of Toomer, Cullen, and Hurston; for, even though each attained artistic stature meriting critical examination of his work, they have received scant attention and even that limited notice has been characterized more often by sociological appraisal than by aesthetic evaluation.

A problem for Afro-American writers is that invariably those who become well-known are condemned or praised for nonaesthetic reasons. If they have written about Afro-Americans, some white critics have expressed hope that, in the future, they would write about the human race. If they have written about human beings who are not black, other critics have condemned them for failing to write about people whom they understood; i.e., Negroes. Sometimes black writers have been castigated merely because they failed to establish themselves as social crusaders or because they removed themselves from the United States. At the other extreme, some black writers have been praised by white critics and readers primarily because they presented literary images which faithfully resembled the images of blacks already fixed in the minds of these white readers.

These practices have not abated. Richard Wright has been derided for using Existentialism, a non-American literary tradition, for choosing to write a novel about white people and for writing about blacks who are not middle-class. Not long ago, white critics denounced James Baldwin for subverting art to the promotion of social crusades for blacks; now, black critics denounce him for betraying his race by seeming to reveal love for white people. One well-known literary figure who could find little to berate in the artistic technique of Pulitzer Prize poet Gwendolyn Brooks concluded his critique by observing that she would remain a minor poet until she selected a broader subject than her present one—the lives and emotions of Afro-Americans. Ralph Ellison, who wrote about blacks, has been castigated by blacks for failing to participate in Civil Rights marches, whereas Frank Yerby, who writes about whites, has been criticized by whites for failing to use his talents to write histories about blacks.

The practice of evaluating Afro-Americans' literary work according to nonliterary criteria is so common that its absurdity becomes apparent only when one considers applying similar criteria to non-Negro authors. Suppose, for instance, that a critic chastized William Faulkner or DuBose Heyward for sometimes writing novels about blacks instead of about their own people. Or that a critic derided Tennessee Williams and Nathaniel Hawthorne as minor and provincial authors because they wrote about Southerners and New Englanders. Or that T. S. Eliot's worth were estimated on the basis of whether or not he was justified in renouncing his American citizenship to become a British subject.

It is regrettable that such absurdity continues today when the literary talent of Afro-Americans has been demonstrated convincingly. The award of the Pulitzer Prize for poetry to Gwendolyn Brooks's *Annie Allen* (1949); the selection of Ralph Ellison's *Invisible Man* (1952) as the most distinguished American novel published from 1939 to 1964; the drama awards to Lorraine Hansberry's *A Raisin in the Sun* (1959) and LeRoi Jones's *Dutchman* (1964), and the Pulitzer Prize for drama to Charles Gordone's *No Place To Be Somebody*, all these attest general respect for the ability of black writers, who today are less likely to be destroyed by social criticism.

The situation was more precarious for earlier black writers, who understood not only that whatever they selected as subject matter would be criticized but also that their works would be evaluated primarily by white readers, who often doubted black writers' ability to create art and who measured verisimilitude according to their own preconceptions of Afro-American character and black-white relationships.

Jean Toomer, Countee Cullen, and Zora Neale Hurston have suffered from aesthetically unsound ap-

praisals of their merits as artists and from myths about
their racial stances. Because the talent of Toomer has
been highly respected, critics have been somewhat sub-
dued in their objections to his decision to live as a white
man rather than as a black; but, knowing little about his
life or work, critics have interpreted his stories and
sketches to fit their conceptions of what a black man
should have thought about black people. For several
years, Countee Cullen continued a debate with critics
who advised him to write as a Negro poet about Negro
subjects. Although he won the debate by changing his
subject, some critics seem pleased to point out that he
wrote less effectively when he abandoned Negro themes.
Zora Neale Hurston alleged that, for several years, she
refused to write a novel because she did not want to write
about the race question but feared that she would be
permitted to write about nothing else. A major objection
to her work has been her silence about issues significant
to Afro-Americans, but an unanswered critical question
is the authenticity of her portrayal of Southern blacks.

This book is intended primarily to rectify the need for
more complete and more objective studies of the works
of these three writers. It is, however, impossible to seg-
regate a study of their works from an examination of
their lives. Living during a time when most black artists
publicly rejoiced in their heritage, each of these three,
in his own way, reacted consciously to his existence—or,
more appropriately, his identification—as a Negro, and
each colored his writing by the nature of his reaction.
In order to analyze and evaluate the works perceptively,
therefore, one must examine them in relation to the
writer's struggle to be whatever he chose—as an artist
and as a human being.

DARWIN T. TURNER

Ann Arbor, Michigan
April 1971

1

Jean Toomer
Exile

When William Dean Howells and *Lyrics of Lowly Life* made Paul Laurence Dunbar famous in 1896, Nathan Eugene Toomer was a two-year-old infant in the home of his grandfather, P. B. S. Pinchback, still remembered as the only known Negro to serve as acting governor of a Southern state. Twenty-five years later, Jean Toomer seemed certain to eclipse the fame of both Dunbar and his own grandfather.

Writers and editors vied with each other to predict his success. Waldo Frank, who became a close friend, marveled about his dramas:

> On the whole, my dear Jean Toomer, I am enormously impressed by the power and fullness and fineness of your Say. . . . A man whose spirit is like yours so high and straight a flame does not need to be told that he has enormous gift.[1]

John McClure, the editor of *Double Dealer*, was the first to publish Toomer's writing. After examining selections, he wrote, "The work which you showed us three weeks ago seems to all of us not only full of rich promise but, to a great extent, of rich fulfillment." [2] About the same time at which Toomer was sending Frank news of this reception, Frank was confessing his humility about his projected book, "Holiday" (1923):

> I am probably presumptuous to write about the Negro, and particularly since I know you who are creating a

1

new phase of American literature (O there's no doubt
of that my friend).[3]

After accepting a story for publication, Lola Ridge,
American editor of *Broom*, boasted that Toomer's work
would endure and would be studied by later generations.[4]

The highest accolades came from Sherwood Anderson, who, having read Toomer's manuscripts in the of-
fice of *Double Dealer*, immediately succumbed to Toomer's verbal magic. Anderson wrote, "Your work is of
special significance to me because it is the first negro
[sic] work I have seen that strikes me as being really
negro." [5] Without mentioning the writings of Dunbar,
Charles Chesnutt, and James Weldon Johnson (or explaining his qualifications for determining the authenticity of "Negro work"), Anderson intensified his praise
a short while later, "You are the only negro . . . who
seems really to have consciously the artist's impulse." [6]

These judgments and predictions were based entirely
on a few poems and sketches, the first of them published
in September 1922. *Cane* (1923), a collection of his
works, increased the number of boosters. Robert Littell
of *The New Review* and Montgomery Gregory of *Opportunity* reviewed it enthusiastically. Allen Tate wrote
to Toomer to praise the genuine and innovative quality
of the technique and the absence of the caricatured
pathos of many whites who wrote about the South.[7]
William Stanley Braithwaite, an Afro-American critic,
exulted,

> in Jean Toomer . . . we come upon the very first
> artist of the race, who with all an artist's passion and
> sympathy for life . . . can write about the Negro
> without the surrender or compromise of the artist's
> vision. . . . *Cane* is a book of gold and bronze, of
> dusk and flame, of ecstasy and pain, and Jean Toomer
> is a bright morning star of a new day of the race in
> literature.[8]

Beneath these paeans, only a few discordant notes were sounded. In a letter to Sherwood Anderson, John McClure hoped that Toomer would not limit himself to realism. Although he believed that Toomer could rise to prominence in realism if he chose, McClure insisted that Toomer's chief talent was lyrical. As a realist, he would be better than most other writers; nevertheless, he would be doing what other talented realists could do as well. By following the African urge and rhapsodizing, however, he would be creating a unique style. In this vein, he could produce his best work and could appear as a commanding and solitary figure among American authors.[9] Anderson also was worried:

> When I saw your work I was thrilled to the toes. Then I thought "he may let the intense white men get him. They are going to color his style, spoil him." I guess that isn't true. You'll stay with your own, won't you? [10]

The worries were justified. Despite his continuing, sometimes desperate efforts during the next twenty-five years, Jean Toomer never again sold a book to publishers.

For a decade publishers and critics remembered his name. Then Depression seized America, and war, and a new generation of writers. Jean Toomer was forgotten except by those who had once read *Cane*. They mourned his silence. Not knowing him, they did not know that he had failed. Certainly they would never have surmised that so talented a writer would be silent unless he desired to be, for *Cane* is not the kind of book for which a writer expends all his talents into one meteoric flame. Ignorant of the letters in which he begged agents and publishers to release his words to the world, the literary cult of Toomer worshippers mourned his silence, and tried vainly to explain the reasons for it. But the only reason they could conjecture seemed so distasteful that once they had uttered it, they relapsed into silent sorrow.

To comprehend the significance of *Cane* and the

frustration attending Toomer's silence, one must look beyond literature into the social and intellectual world of
America during the twenties and thirties. In that generation, many Afro-Americans agreed with W. E. B. Du-
Bois and James Weldon Johnson that intellectual and
artistic achievements would elevate the status of the
race. Benjamin Brawley and Carter Woodson unearthed
and publicized the major and minor contributions of
black politicians, scientists, artists, musicians, writers, and
educators. Charles Johnson, editor of *Opportunity*, and
Alain Locke of Howard sought out promising Afro-American writers to present to America. Such a sustained
effort to identify artistically and intellectually talented
Afro-Americans increased Jean Toomer's importance
among Negro historians. They could commend him
without any fear that critics would accuse them of ex-
aggerating his ability. He was a talented artist, and he
was nationally acclaimed. Even more important, as the
historians of literature knew, Anderson's evaluation was
accurate. In 1923 Toomer was the most talented Negro
writer America had bred.

In the thirties and even the forties, therefore, the
mourning over Toomer's silence was loud because the
voices of those who regretted the loss of literary contributions were joined by the voices of those who regretted
the loss of a weapon in a sociological battle. But the
mourning was embittered by the suspicion that the actual reason for Toomer's silence further demeaned the
race: that the fair-skinned Toomer had repudiated the
race, had married a wealthy woman, and had disappeared
into the mainstream of America. Respect for his talent
sustained his memory, but conflicting feelings of envy
and bitterness toward the man provoked comments
which run the gamut of the emotional scale. At one end
is the amused or indifferent tone of those who congratu-
lated him for being able to escape the difficulties of living

as a black man in America. At the other is the strident
tone of those who alleged that he lost his ability to write
when he ceased being a Negro. The moderate tone is suggested by Robert Bone, who believed that Toomer
stopped writing because *Cane* proved to be an economic
failure.[11]

Truth is complex when it must be surmised from
letters and notes, and when that truth itself is partially
submerged in the emotions of a writer who cannot see
it clearly. Nevertheless, the shadow, the outline at least,
of truth about Jean Toomer can be discerned sufficiently.
His failure was predictable. Outwardly, he was a man
who immediately impressed people as an individual pre-
destined to succeed. Tall, handsome, gifted with what
Arna Bontemps has described as an hypnotic voice, confident in manner, and talented as musician, writer, and
lecturer, he, like Richard Cory, glittered when he walked.
Inwardly, despite his belief, or prayer, that he would be
great,[12] Toomer was an exile, a Flying Dutchman, vainly
searching for a haven in which he might moor.

To understand *Cane* fully and to explain the reasons
for Toomer's subsequent failures as a writer, one therefore must look into his life.

He remembered his childhood as lonely.[13] Born December 26, 1894, in Washington, D.C., Nathan Eugene
Toomer was still an infant when his father, Nathan
Toomer of Georgia, deserted his mother, Nina, and she
returned to the family home ruled by the legendary
P. B. S. Pinchback. His earliest memories were of bitter
quarrels between his mother and his grandfather, who,
having opposed her marriage, frequently reminded her of
her errors. When his mother moved to New York in
1905, Toomer blamed his grandfather for forcing her to
escape. Soon afterwards, she married again, and the
Pinchbacks joined her. They were accompanied to Brook-
lyn by young Eugene Pinchback—as the family called

him in an effort to obliterate all memory of his father. But Eugene remained lonely. Unable to feel close to the stranger his mother had married and believing that she had betrayed him, he yearned for the father he had never known. In 1909 his mother died following an appendectomy,[14] and Eugene returned to Washington with his grandfather, whom he blamed for his father's disappearance and for his mother's remarriage and death. In his need, he turned to his grandmother, Nina Emily. But few grandmothers can provide the intellectual companionship and the understanding required by a teen-aged boy. Nina Emily could not. She gave love, which he returned, but she could not help with the new questions for which he was forced to find his own answers.

The return to Washington in 1909 thrust Toomer for the first time into an Afro-American neighborhood and school. Previously, he had lived among people indifferent to their varying shades of complexion. Now, gangs of black youths fought against gangs of whites, and called him to join them. But, identifying himself with both groups, he could join neither.

Sex too troubled the teen-ager. Believing himself in love, newly aware of sexual desires but unwilling to gratify them with girls of his group, superstitiously fearful that his body would weaken unless he experienced intercourse, envious of other youths who boasted of their conquests, unable to discuss his dilemma, Toomer behaved in a manner already characterizing his response to any situation which he could not dominate. He contemptuously withdrew from his friends. In isolation he dedicated himself to developing his body through diet and exercise.

During the six years following graduation from high school, Toomer pathetically retraced a single pattern as he desperately searched for permanent interests. Repeatedly, he excited himself with a new career, pursued it frantically, then abruptly withdrew and returned despondently to Washington to a baffled and increasingly irate grandfather.

During the summer and fall of 1914 he studied agriculture at the University of Wisconsin, a choice of study which Toomer could never explain, but which may have germinated either in a rebellion against the urban, capitalistic life represented by his grandfather or in an effort to enter the gentleman-planter class with which he identified his father. Fearing alienation if he were identified as Negro, Toomer for the first time assumed the racial stance which became permanent. He volunteered nothing about his ancestry; if questioned, he responded enigmatically. Quickly proving Northern college students incapable of resisting his charm, Toomer earned a nomination for presidency of the freshman class; but, convinced that he could not defeat the candidate supported by campus fraternities, he withdrew from the race. Then, suspecting that his former followers rejected him because he had disappointed them, Toomer withdrew from their society and, at the close of the first term, withdrew from school.[15]

Although he had disliked agricultural studies at the University of Wisconsin, the next fall Toomer applied to the Massachusetts College of Agriculture; but, peeved because his transcripts from the University of Wisconsin did not arrive before registration, he left the school.

Having been interested in physical development since childhood, he decided to enroll in the American College of Physical Training in Chicago in February 1916. The following autumn, bored by the lack of intellectual stimulation, he also matriculated in a premedical program at the University of Chicago. Even before difficulties with biology quickly dissuaded him from the projected medical career, he had darted in another direction.

A lecture by Clarence Darrow during the summer of

1916 had not only converted him from lukewarm faith in Catholicism and capitalism to enthusiastic endorsement of atheism and socialism, but had inspired him to want to teach others—or at least to be applauded. Now, having lost interest in his own studies, he offered evening lectures on philosophy and economics in classrooms at the university. The close of the first term and the lack of money, however, forced the customary winter retreat to the Pinchback home in Washington. There, a reading of Lester Ward's *Dynamic Sociology* propelled him to New York University to study sociology in the summer of 1917. But, fascinated by a visiting historian from the City College of New York, he decided that he preferred history; consequently, in the fall, he followed his piper to CCNY. Other historians were less charming, he soon learned; and they were his teachers. His interests already were winking in the direction of psychology when events outside the ivied walls dispelled all thoughts of study.

America was at war. Toomer did not want to go to war; he preferred remaining in school. But he was so certain that he would be summoned before completing the year that he angrily withdrew from school. When his physical examination revealed poor eyesight and a hernia, Toomer became piqued because the army did not want the services which he had not wanted to give. Consequently, he immediately tried to enlist in the Red Cross and the Y.M.C.A., but neither wanted the former student of the American College of Physical Training.[16]

Unable to return to school in New York, but unwilling to return to Grandfather Pinchback, Toomer drifted back to Chicago, where he sold automobiles for a Ford dealer. Soon he secured a position as a substitute director of physical education in a school near Milwaukee. There he read extensively in the works of George Bernard Shaw, whom he later credited with having made him aware of literary style and having introduced him to the intellectual life.[17]

After the month or two of teaching ended, Toomer retreated to Washington for the customary winter hibernation and nursing of the wounds. Unable to endure his grandfather's reproaches, however, Toomer, like his mother before him, fled to New York, where he relocated himself as a white-collar clerk at the Acker, Merrall, and Conduit grocery company. Continually adding activities, Toomer soon built a daily schedule of music lessons, practice as a writer, work in the grocery company, supervision of physical education at a settlement house on the East Side, and occasional discussions of socialism with the boys of the settlement house. After five months of the strenuous schedule, he collapsed physically and retired to a farm in Ellenville, New York, to regain his health. There he found sufficient time for writings, which earned a measure of respect from his grandfather even though they earned him no money.

When Jean Toomer returned to Washington in the summer of 1919, Pinchback helped him secure a job. He believed that Toomer was finally ready to settle down, even if only in the uncertain career of a writer. But almost before Toomer had unpacked his bag, he was repacking to join a former classmate for a vacation which his grandfather doubted that he needed.

When Toomer drifted back to Washington that fall, jobless and penniless, a disenchanted grandfather voiced the thoughts rehearsed during the summer. Weary of the reproaches, Toomer hitchhiked through snow to New York. This time he took a job as a shipyard laborer in order to gain among the working classes the practical experience which he considered necessary to his work as a socialistic reformer.

The winter of 1919 was scarcely the time to launch a campaign for socialism. Terrorized by rumors about communistic revolution in America, threatened by strikes in the steel and coal industries, the controlling forces in America viewed suspiciously anyone who did not praise

democracy and big business. They need not have feared
Toomer, however, even if they had known his thoughts.
Ten days in a shipyard persuaded him that the working
classes lacked the acumen to appreciate or to deserve his
missionary efforts. Instead of discussing socialism, they
merely wanted to gamble and to make love. With some
disappointment and considerable relief, Toomer retreated to the white-collar slavery of the grocery firm,
which was beginning to demonstrate almost as much
patience as his grandfather. He was released from his
slavery, however, when six hundred dollars netted from
his grandfather's sale of his mother's house afforded him
time to write and to luxuriate in a literary crowd in New
York.

The actual beginning of Jean Toomer, writer, probably
can be dated from this time, the spring of 1920. While
chasing many gleams, he had read extensively in atheism,
naturalism, socialism, sociology, psychology, and the
dramas of Shaw. To these scientific, philosophical, and
social writings, he had added *Wilhelm Meister* of
Goethe, the romances of Victor Hugo, and the verse
of Walt Whitman. After his abortive crusade in the shipyard, he had reaccepted capitalism as a necessary evil.
Dismayed because his atheism had shocked a Quaker
girl, he had reaffirmed his faith in God and in religion,
even though he refused to believe in orthodox creeds and
churches.[18] Introduced now to a literary world of such
people as Lola Ridge, Edwin Arlington Robinson, and
Waldo Frank, he was dazzled with the prospect of retir-
ing from arid philosophies into a cultural aristocracy.

Looking back from a diary written in 1930, he saw the
Toomer of the early twenties as a vanity-burdened poseur
who adopted the manners of a poet, a poet's appearance,
and a French-sounding name—Jean. A more objective observer sees a seriously confused young man of twenty-five,
who was not content to be average, but who had discov-

ered nothing at which to be great; who wanted to guide, to instruct, to lead, to dominate, but who would withdraw completely if he could not; and who habitually discontinued studies with startling abruptness, not because he had mastered them, but because he had lost interest or, as with music, had decided that he could not become a master. This, however, was the tortured soul hidden by the ever present mask of intellect, confidence, and charm which caused Waldo Frank to write, "You are one of those men one must see but once to know the timbre and the truth of." [19]

When he had exhausted the six hundred dollars, Toomer returned to Washington to spend the next year working at the Howard Theatre and preparing himself for a career as an author. His reading was amazingly varied: Waldo Frank, Dostoevsky, Tolstoy, Flaubert, Baudelaire, Sinclair Lewis, Theodore Dreiser, American poets, Coleridge, Blake, Pater, Freud, Buddhist philosophy, Eastern teachings, occultism, the Bible, Robert Frost, Sherwood Anderson, *Dial, Poetry, Liberator, The Nation, The New Republic.* Although he later asserted that he destroyed most that he wrote during the period, he preserved one play, "Natalie Mann," completed by February 1922, and fragments of an autobiographical novel.

In both works, although he censured the hypocritical, repressive morality of middle-class Negroes and advanced his philosophy that successful individuals are those who have won freedom and integrity for their souls, Toomer pleaded for Afro-Americans as he would never do in fiction again. In "Natalie Mann," he attributed the restrictive morality and superficial values of middle-class Negroes to their misguided attempts to conform to the false morality of the American white man. He accused American white men of debauching black women and of crushing the artistic, political, and industrial careers of all

black people who are sensitive to pain. In the extant fragments of his autobiographical novel, he is even more
acerbic. Harry Kenton, an Afro-American who is darker
in color than Eugene Stanton (Toomer's self-portrait),
curses America: "My family has been here for generations. But they're colored. They're not Americans yet.
Any cockeyed louse with a white skin can come over here
from lousy Europe and become an American. I can't."
Rebelling against this society which rejects him, Ken deliberately refuses to conform to the acceptable patterns.[20]

As an artist, however, Toomer had not yet mastered
his craft. His attempt in "Natalie Mann" is impressive.
Instead of imitating the representational dramas fashion-
able on the American stage, he experimented with expressionistic drama. The characters are posited for types
of mankind. Natalie Mann represents the middle-class
Negro woman inhibited by parental morality enforced
by social disapproval. Nathan Merilh, Toomer's self-
portrait, is a Messiah, who must sacrifice himself in order
to effect the release of Natalie's soul. Etta, a friend of
Nathan, embodies the more primitive African spirit, innately free from intraracial repression and interracial cor-
ruption. In stylized phrasing rather than realistic dialogue, Toomer mimicked the banality of middle-class
devotees of pseudo culture or lyrically expressed the intensity of uninhibited souls. He designed the setting sug-
gestively rather than realistically. A portrait on the wall
of Nathan's study symbolizes a blend of the mind of
Western man (represented by Tolstoy) with the soul of
the African. And Toomer accorded dance an importance
it had never known in American drama. Dance is not
merely a rhythmic expression of the soul; it becomes the
medium through which the soul releases itself from social restrictions. No American dramatist except Eugene
O'Neill had dared to experiment so unconventionally.

The intention, however, surpasses the achievement.

The plot is too slight to sustain a spectator's interest. After acceding to society's demands that she end her romance with Nathan Merilh, Natalie defies society by becoming his mistress. Although she consequently totters her first step toward self-realization, she cannot complete the process until she has freed herself from dependence upon Nathan. She achieves this final stage only when, watching Nathan collapse at the climax of a soul-releasing dance, she realizes that he is a god.

More disturbing than the slight plot is the vague thought. Toomer had not learned, and never would learn, to translate his philosophy into an idiom comprehensible to the uninitiated. Furthermore, Toomer's satirical use of language is too subtle. It confused even the literature-sophisticated Waldo Frank, who assumed that the dull, banal speeches of the middle-class guardians of morality were artistic ineptitudes rather than cleverly contrived mimickings.

The fragments of the autobiographical novel reveal greater artistic sureness. The characters are credible and provocative; Toomer modeled them on his friends. The tone is more consistently effective because it remains in the lyric key which Toomer wrote well. And the thought is less pompous because, instead of using the literary form as a thinly disguised platform for his moral preaching, Toomer concentrated upon sympathetic delineation of two young people frustrated by their existences as Negroes. Unfortunately, however, only fragments exist: one episode depicting the frustration of Harry Kenton's father, one episode exploring the mind of Harry himself, and one episode describing Eugene Stanton's efforts to comfort the girl with whom he shares the quest for sexual satisfaction.

A trip to Georgia in the fall of 1921 provided Toomer with additional material about his major interest at the moment—the Afro-American. As an acting principal in

Sparta, Georgia, Toomer learned the folk songs, the folktales, and the folkways of Southern blacks. After three months he returned to Washington in November. Inspired, he feverishly began writing poems and sketches about the South, especially women of the South. Eight months later he admitted to Frank that he had drained himself,[21] but by that time he had completed most of the sketches and poems on which his reputation rests. In September 1922, *Double Dealer* published "Storm Ending," a poem, and *Liberator* published "Carma," a short story. By the end of the year, *Broom* had accepted a sketch, and the *Modern Review* had requested material. In January 1923, Boni and Liveright sent him a contract for the publication of *Cane*. Jean Toomer seemed to have found himself at last.

Cane inspires critical rhapsodies rather than analysis. As Robert Bone wrote, "A critical analysis of *Cane* is a frustrating task, for Toomer's art, in which 'outlines are reduced to essences,' is largely destroyed in the process of restoration. No paraphrase can properly convey the aesthetic pleasure derived from a sensitive reading of *Cane*." [22]

It is not a novel, not even the experimental novel for which Bone pleaded to justify including it in his study of novels by Negroes.[23] It is, instead, a collection of character sketches, short stories, poems, and a play, which forms one of the distinguished achievements in the writings of Americans. The first section of the book is composed of sketches, stories, and poems based on life—especially the life of Afro-American women—in Georgia. The stories of the second section, located in Washington and Chicago, were written to bring the collection to a length respectable for publication in book form. The third section is a drama set in Georgia.

Toomer's supreme talent in his best prose work is the ability to suggest character lyrically. Restricting his vision to one or two traits of personality, he tells a story intended merely to help the reader perceive the individual.

Six women are the focus of the first section, the most appealing part of *Cane*. One is Karintha, who personifies the physical beauty for which men yearn:

> Men had always wanted her, this Karintha, even as a child, Karintha carrying beauty, perfect as dusk when the sun goes down . . .[24]

> Karintha, at twelve, was a wild flash that told the other folks just what it was to live. At sunset, when there was no wind, and the pine-smoke from over by the sawmill hugged the earth, and you couldn't see more than a few feet in front, her sudden darting past you was a bit of vivid color, like a black bird that flashes in light. . . . Already, rumors were out about her.[25]

Then,

> Karintha is a woman, and she has had a child. A child fell out of her womb onto a bed of pine-needles in the forest. Pine-needles are smooth and sweet. They are elastic to the feet of rabbits.[26]

> Karintha at twenty, carrying beauty, perfect as dusk when the sun goes down. Karintha. . . .[27]

Five pages. Karintha, a beautiful child whom old men ride hobby horse. Karintha at twelve—beautiful, matured to sexual knowledge, no longer permitting herself to be dandled on the knees of old men. Karintha at twenty— often mated, supported by men, mother of an unwanted child who died unwanted on the pine needles beneath the smoke curling from a sawmill. Karintha—"Men do not know that the soul of her was a growing thing ripened too soon. They will bring their money; they will die not having found it out." [28]

As "Karintha" typifies Toomer's style, so the protagonist typifies his women. Elizabeth Loguen complained about the unreality of his female characters. They all love, she believed, as Toomer thought women should.[29] Perhaps this judgment is accurate. Each in her own way is an elusive beauty, who charitably or indifferently or inquisitively offers her body to men who will never understand her soul. Each portrait haunts the reader as the woman haunted the narrator, who seeks the soul, the feminine essence of women who in less artistic works would be pitied or castigated as social outcasts.

> Becky was the white woman who had two Negro sons. She's dead; they've gone away. The pines whisper to Jesus. The Bible flaps its leaves with an aimless rustle on her mound.[30]

Becky is a pariah. "Becky had one Negro son. Who gave it to her? Damn buck nigger, said the white folks' mouths. She wouldn't tell." [31]

Cast out by God, cast out by white folks, cast out by black folks, Becky lives alone, unseen. Five years later her son appears in town carrying a baby. " 'Becky has another son,' was what the whole town knew. But nothing was said, for the part of man that says things to the likes of that had told itself that if there was a Becky, that Becky now was dead." [32]

The boys grow, sullen and cunning. They drift; they fight; they leave. Only smoke curling from the chimney tells that Becky lives there still.

Sunday. The blue sheen God with one eye rushes by the cabin. The chimney falls into the cabin, falls to the floor in a mound of bricks. "Becky, if she was there, lay under them." [33]

There is Fern.

Face flowed into her eyes. Flowed in soft cream foam and plaintive ripples, in such a way that wherever your glance may momentarily have rested, it immediately thereafter wavered in the direction of her eyes. . . . They were strange eyes. In this, that they sought nothing—that is nothing that was obvious and tangible and that one could see, and they gave the impression that nothing was to be denied. . . . Fern's eyes desired nothing that you could give her; there was no reason why they should withhold. Men saw her eyes and fooled themselves. Fern's eyes said to them that she was easy. When she was young, a few men took her but got no joy from it. And then, once done, they felt bound to her. . . . felt as though it would take them a lifetime to fulfill an obligation which they could find no name for. They became attached to her, and hungered after finding the barest trace of what she might desire.[34]

When, weary of men's bodies, she rejected them, the men of the town transformed her into The Virgin.

The narrator also experiences the peculiar, unselfish desire to help her. But, when he holds her in his arms, she is tortured with something that can get out only "in plaintive, convulsive sounds, mingled with calls to Christ Jesus. And then she sang, brokenly. A Jewish Cantor singing with a broken voice." [35]

"Nothing ever really happened. Nothing ever can to Fern, not even I. Something I would do for her, some fine unnamed thing." [36] Fernie May Rosen, with Semitic nose, cream-foam face, and eyes into which God "flowed in as I've seen the countryside flow in." [37]

Carma's tale is the crudest melodrama. Her husband's in the gang [chaingang]. And it's her fault he got there. Working with a contractor, he was away most of the time. She had others. No one blames her for that.[38]

When her husband accused her of infidelity, she, carrying a gun, fled hysterically from the house and into the cane-brake. He feared to follow, until the sound of the gun and the silence told him that she had shot herself. Summoning assistance from neighbors, he searched for her, and they found her. She was not dead.

> Twice deceived, and one deception proved the other. His head went off. Slashed one of the men who'd helped, the man who'd stumbled over her. Now he's in the gang. Who was her husband. Should she not take others, this Carma, strong as a man . . . ?[39]

Esther's story is four days in eighteen years. Nine years old, Esther—hair falling in soft curls about her high cheek-boned, chalk-white face, too serious, too flat and dead for a girl of nine—Esther sees King Barlo, who has fallen into a trance. She listens to him preach his visions of a black giant chained by white-ant biddies:

> "They led him to the coast, they led him to the sea, they led him across the ocean and they didn't set him free. The old coast didn't miss him, and the new coast wasn't free, he left the old-coast brothers, to give birth to you and me. . . ."
> He became the starting point of the only living patterns that her mind was to know.[40]

Sixteen years old, "Esther begins to dream" of whooping, clanging fire engines saving her dimpled child; of another fire, dampened only by the gallons of tobacco juice squirted by chewing loafers; of women fleeing from the fire, skirts raised above their heads, ludicrous underclothes displayed; and of her baby—black, singed, woolly, tobacco-juice baby.

Twenty-two years old, schooling ended, near-white Esther—too white for the blacks, too black for the whites—works in her father's store and dreams of King Barlo, who will return and be her love.

Twenty-seven years old, her hair "dull silk on puny corn ears," her face pale as "gray dust that dances with dead cotton leaves," Esther sees King Barlo for the first time in eighteen years. He is big, flaming black, and rich; she is lonely, unable to repress her dreams of pale flames. At midnight, her mind, "solid, contained, and blank as a sheet of darkened ice," she rushes past the flaming windows to a tavern, where she tells King Barlo that she has come for him. He is drunk, lustful, ugly. "She draws away, frozen. . . . There is no air, no street, and the town has completely disappeared." [41]

The most fully developed, but least successful story of the first section is "Blood-Burning Moon." It is the tale of Louisa, "color of oak leaves on young trees in fall; . . . breast, firm and up-pointed like ripe acorns"; Louisa, apex of a triangle whose other angles are her two lovers—white Bob Stone, son of her employers, and black Tom Burwell. Lyric and perceptive while exploring the mind of Louisa, while examining Bob's futile efforts to analyze his Southern attitudes and his interest in Louisa, or while describing scene and movement, Toomer faltered when he attempted to imitate Southern dialect.

Offended that the woman he wants would make love with a black man, Bob Stone goes to Louisa's home, where he finds her in the arms of Tom. Incapable of defeating Tom physically, he draws a knife; but Tom, skilled at such fighting, cuts Bob's throat. In self-defense, Tom has killed a white man. For this, he is burned to death beneath the blood-burning moon.

Faintly reminiscent of Gertrude Stein, Waldo Frank, and Sherwood Anderson, these portraits, nevertheless, are the work of an artist possessing an individualized style.[42] The style depends upon contrasting images of man and nature: the vivid color of Karintha, a November cotton flower, against the pine-needles and pine smoke; Becky, visible only through her dark children, against the blue-sheen locomotive god; white-skinned Esther against flames and tobacco juice. It depends upon lyric language, deceptively smooth and simple, the language of a poet careful of words.

The dominant contrast between the Georgia section of *Cane* and the Northern section is between a natural response to sexual drives and a self-conscious, frustrating inability to realize oneself. The women of section one respond naturally and instinctively to their urges, regardless of the attitudes of society. Only near-white Esther experiences frustrating conflicts, and she is the unhappiest of the women. Even in the first part of *Cane*, Toomer pointed to the tensions and deliberate self-delusions arising in reaction to natural behavior. People refuse to see the wickedness of young Karintha; they tell themselves that Becky must be dead; they transform Fern into The Virgin. Townspeople can accept aberrants only by pretending that there has been no deviation from the socially acceptable. The tragedy resulting from the failure to sustain delusion proves the inability of people to accept the reality of natural sex drives: Carma's husband kills a man when he is forced to realize that Carma has taken lovers in his absence; Bob Stone attacks Tom Burwell when he is forced to realize that Louisa has given herself to a black man.

In Washington and Chicago, delusion becomes reality, will represses action, and natural self-realization becomes impossible. In two of the four stories, conflict arises between a primitive being—instinctively, shamelessly seeking gratification and realization—and a society-sophisticated being—repressed, frustrated, unable to forget the image he seeks to preserve. In the other two, "Bona and Paul" and "Theatre," protagonists are frustrated by their tensions, by the conflict between will and desire.

"Avey" pictures a Northern Karintha. Offered professional opportunities impossible for Fern or Karintha,

Avey listlessly, bovinely loses them and accepts, in their stead, her lovers' lust. Unable to understand or approve her aimlessness, the narrator vainly tries first to change her, then to meet her upon her own level. Having failed to mate with her spiritually or physically, he, like a saint, holds her in his arms and meditates about the innocence of the "orphan-woman."

"Box-Seat" tells of Dan Moore, whose dreams of being a militant Messiah fade into his impotence. Frustrated because Muriel, a school teacher, resists his impassioned advances, and infuriated by a world that categorizes people as the accepted or the freaks, Dan challenges the tradition of that world, but forgets that he has offered the challenge.

"Bona and Paul" is located in Chicago, where the two protagonists attend a college of physical education. Paul Johnson is Negro; Bona is white and Southern-bred. After striving to repress their mutual attraction, they yield during ecstatic dancing. Too self-conscious, however, they cannot realize themselves spiritually or physically. Seeing mockery in the eyes of a black doorman, Paul pauses to assure the man that he and Bona are going outside for spiritual rather than physical consummation. By the time Paul reaches the street, Bona has disappeared.

Although both central characters of "Theatre" are Afro-American, they stand on different social levels. John is the brother of a theater manager. Dorris is a dancer. Despite their mutual attraction, neither can free himself sufficiently to translate desire into action. Dorris tries to express her feelings by dancing before him. But John's mind is "contained above desire of his body. He wills thought to rid his mind of passion." [43] Fearing that Dorris will ridicule him if he relinquishes this self-control, he dreams of their union, but he does not act.

Longer than the earlier stories of *Cane*, "Theatre," "Box-Seat," and "Bona and Paul" reveal the weaknesses that restricted Toomer as a short-story writer and, later, as a novelist. They end vaguely and inconclusively. The perceptively sketched characters act and react; but the narrator then walks away from them. The material remains amorphous—a disappointment to a reader persuaded to expect more than a sketch.

Jean Toomer often transformed his personal experiences into universally meaningful criticisms of life. Like the narrator of "Avey," he had loved a high school girl who had been interested only in college men. He had shuddered when his less sensitive high school friends had described in detail their actual or exaggerated conquests. He too had attended college in Wisconsin, although not as long as the narrator, had hitchhiked to New York, had bruised his vanity in unsuccessful job hunts, had loved a girl at Harper's Ferry, and had tried to change her. Like John, the brother of the theater manager, he had worked in a theater; and, even earlier, led by his uncle, he had played stage-door Johnny to older women of the chorus line. Like Paul Johnson, he had attended a school for physical training in Chicago, had writhed before stares of white people whom he imagined to be speculating about his racial identity, and had loved a white girl whose family opposed her relationship with a Negro. These three stories, therefore, contain the truth of imagination based upon reality. They reveal the frustrations of Jean Toomer.

Set against the stories of part one, however, they point to a more universal thought. The educated Toomer, like John, interposed will between desire and action. Consequently, he lived mainly in fantasies and dreams. In contrast, the Beckys and the Karinthas realize themselves by acting according to instinct. These later stories, therefore, express a regret that a male cannot live as instinctively as a female can, and suggest a yearning for a more primitive existence in which desire, not will, can be the ruling force.

If Toomer conceived this existence to be most nearly achieved by Afro-Americans in the South, he saw that even there a restrictive society censured those who obeyed natural urges. Furthermore, unlike Sherwood Anderson and some of the followers of the van Vechten vogue, he noted unhappily that Southern blacks themselves were rapidly losing the innocence of Eden by substituting will and social image for the purity of freedom and naturalness.

"Kabnis" is the longest work in *Cane*. Although Toomer tried to have a revised version produced as a play, Kenneth Macgowan rejected it because it lacked a plot. A producer might be more charitable in these days of the Theatre of the Absurd. Like Samuel Beckett's *Waiting for Godot*, it is a spectacle of futility; like Ionesco's *The Chairs*, it substitutes a meaningless whimper for the anticipated climactic explosion. "Kabnis," however, is not developed as artistically as either of these. Toomer failed to focus the multitudinous rays of light into one clear beam.

The slight plot sets an inhibited and impotent Northerner among Southerners who have failed to achieve self-realization. Choosing to remain in the South, he becomes an apprentice in a blacksmith shop. Among his people in their ancestral home, he seeks to realize himself; but, because of his moral weakness, he finds only drunkenness, debauchery, and impotence.

Superseding the plot is the theme Toomer attempted to express through allegorical characters. The protagonist Ralph Kabnis represents the contemporary Northern-born, educated Afro-American searching for his identity. Although he has pilgrimaged to the region which he posits for his ancestral home, he cannot fully identify with any of his race who live successfully in that region. He cannot merge with uneducated blacks because they discern his cultural dissimilarities. Kabnis despises men of the mold of Hanby, a principal, who represents one type

of middle-class Southern Negro. Deferential toward
white people, Hanby abuses blacks to compensate for the
humiliation which he experiences in relationships with
white people. Trained to respect formal education, Kabnis cannot imitate Halsey, who represents the semiskilled
worker. Disdaining formal education because it fails to
improve lives of Afro-Americans, Halsey derives enjoy-
ment and pride from laboring with his hands. Although
he, like Hanby, treats white people deferentially, he considers himself their intellectual equal. Nor can Kabnis
assume the indifference of Layman, who represents the
intelligent, but untrained clergy of the South. A self-
appointed teacher and minister, Layman observes mental
and physical indignities inflicted upon the black man,
but he preserves his own life by remaining silent. Although he knows the impotence of the primitive religion
he teaches, he offers its fervor as a drug to help his race
forget the painful reality of their existence.

Because Kabnis is intellectual rather than physical, he
cannot mate with Stella, a personification of the sensual
female. Stella's mother was abused by white men; she
herself has been used by black leaders. Nor can Kabnis
do more than dream romantically of union with Halsey's
sister Carrie K, the Madonna figure who responds to
Lewis but represses her desire. Kabnis must mate with
Cora, who is as flat mentally as she is physically. Neither
sensual nor intellectual nor spiritual, she imitates and she
exists.

Weak, debauched, impotent, betrayed by his faith in
education and in religion, Kabnis awaits a message from
Father John, symbol of the Afro-American ancestor, the
maker of spirituals, the voice of the past. But Father
John, aged and infirm, speaks rarely and unintelligibly.
When at last he gathers the clarity and force to pro-
nounce a judgment from the past, he merely mutters, "O
th sin th white folks 'mitted when they made th Bible

lie." As Horatio says, "There needs no ghost . . . come from the grave to tell us this."

The story ends inconclusively but with pessimistically suggestive irony. After a night of debauchery and disappointment, Kabnis, carrying a bucket of dead coals, climbs the stairs to begin his labor as apprentice blacksmith. Behind him, in the cellar, Carrie K kneels before Father John and prays for Jesus to return.[44] The virgin child prays before a deaf, blind, and senile savior. Meanwhile, Kabnis, who is unfit to be a laborer, carries the ashes of dreams into his apprenticeship for a trade which is soon to be obsolete.

The only ray of optimism in the allegory of impotence and nonrealization is Lewis, a Christ figure, who is what a stronger Kabnis might have been. Northern-born, educated, capable of acting according to emotional impulse or of controlling his emotion by will power, Lewis has come South for a month to observe and to communicate with his people. Compassionate and perceptive, he attempts to assist them, but he is driven away when they imbibe the anodynes of sex and alcohol.

Although critics, following Waldo Frank's suggestion in the introduction to *Cane*, have written of Toomer as a poet, the most accurate statement is that he was a prose lyricist. He bridged the stories of *Cane* with poems, but generally his most successful poems are those which develop the themes of the stories. His poetry is a succession of images; its rhythm emerges from image rather than accent or sound.

Probably the most successful of the independent poems are "Song of the Son" and "Georgia Dusk." "Song of the Son" might have been the prologue to *Cane*, for it expresses Toomer's vision of the South:

> *O land and soil, red soil and sweet-gum tree*
> *So scant of grass, so profligate of pines,*

Now, just before an epoch's sun declines
Thy son, in time, I have returned to thee,
Thy son, in time, I have returned to thee.

In time, for though the sun is setting on
A sun-lit race of slaves, it has not set;
Though late, O soil, it is not too late yet
To catch thy plaintive soul, leaving, soon gone,
Leaving, to catch thy plaintive soul soon gone.[45]

"Georgia Dusk" is an epilogue, capturing the reddening sky, the blue smoke curling from the sawdust pile of the closing mill, and the songs of the men whose racial memories picture kings and caravans.

Most of the poems, however, are exquisite only in the sharpness and suggestiveness of their imagery. For instance, "Storm Ending":

Thunder blossoms gorgeously above our heads,
Great, hollow, bell-like flowers,
Rumbling in the wind,
Stretching clappers to strike our ears . . .
Full-lipped flowers
Bitten by the sun
Bleeding rain
Dripping rain like golden honey—
And the sweet earth flying from the thunder.[46]

Or the more critical "Georgia Portrait":

Hair—braided chesnut,
        coiled like a lyncher's rope,
Eyes—fagots,
Lips—old scars, or the first red blisters,
Breath—the last sweet scent of cane,
And her slim body, white as the ash
        of black flesh after flame.[47]

From a vantage point forty years later it is possible to discern limitations in *Cane*. First, Toomer's canvas is limited. Except in "Kabnis," Toomer did not interpret the Southern black. He wrote lyrically about Southern women isolated or destroyed because they have ignored society's restrictions on sexual behavior. In "Natalie Mann" he had argued for such rebellion; in the first part of *Cane*, he described the results with sympathetic awareness that tragedy eventuates as long as society itself erects taboos. Having matured too quickly, Karintha prostitutes herself. Becky is alienated from white and black because she, a white woman, has mated with a black. Children, the natural result of sexual action, are unwanted because they prove the fact which otherwise might be ignored. Unwanted, they are murdered or become murderers. Angered by Carma's adultery and humiliated by her deceit, Carma's husband tries to kill her. Louisa, who took two lovers—one white, one black—loses both. Fern—half-black, half-white—gropes for a spiritual realization which she does not discover in the physical realities of sexual intercourse. Half-white, sex-starved, Esther is forced from her world of sexual fantasies. Both Fern and Esther withdraw from reality—Fern into mystic vision, Esther into Freudian fantasy. Most of Toomer's Northern women know even less happiness than the Southern ones, for they fear to admit their desires.

Toomer could not build a career upon lyric presentations of such women. But he had little else to offer. His male figures are stereotypes, personifications, and reproductions of his satiric, self-pitying, or idealized image of himself. At his best, he did not tell stories; he sang and painted, and his subject was Woman.

An additional weakness appears in the stories located in Washington and Chicago. Toomer shifted from the stance of sympathetic observer or recorder of the tale of folk; he joined in the dance. Lewis replaced Kabnis. The

change of point of view was unfortunate. Whereas Toomer could sing of women, he could not write effectively
about Jean Toomer. Toomer, the character, is a neurotic,
vanity-driven figure, like Paul in "Bona and Paul." Or he
is a somewhat pompous, ineffectual reformer of souls,
like the nameless narrator of "Avey." Or he is a god, like
Nathan Merilh of "Natalie Mann" and like the protagonists of most of the stories Toomer wrote subsequently.

John McClure perceived both Toomer's talent and his
potential weakness when he explained to Anderson that
Toomer faltered when he tried to write realistic dialogue.
As a lyricist, Toomer succeeded only when he expressed
the feelings of the characters in his own words either in
quotation or in indirect discourse.[48] Toomer's gift was the
ability to write from within himself, but he could not use
that gift effectively when writing about himself. He
needed to balance his subjectivity with the objective attempt to create someone other than himself.

The third unheeded warning of impending disaster in
Cane is Toomer's substitution of satire for sympathy.
Part of the reason can be traced to Toomer's contrasting
attitudes about his relationship to the characters in the
tales. He had identified himself temperamentally with
the Southern blacks. As he wrote while he was preparing
the lyrics for *Cane*,

> My seed was planted in the cane-and-cotton fields, and
> in the souls of black and white people in the small
> southern town. My seed was planted in myself down
> there.[49]

Although allowance must be made for the characteristic
enthusiasm with which Toomer embraced every new interest, whether sociology or the black field hand, much
of this feeling was genuine. It is also true, however, that
consciously or subconsciously Toomer knew that he, like
Lewis, was visiting in the South. Thus, he could write

sympathetically as one who feels kinship yet maintains artistic detachment. He desired merely to observe, to sense, and to reflect the milieu, not to change it.

When he wrote of Washington and Chicago, however, he lost his detachment. He wanted to reform the people to rid them of their indolence or their anxieties or their inhibitions. Consequently his tone became sharper, sardonic, satirical. Avey, he lamented, is too much like a cow. She lives by instinct, with few drives and fewer goals. Yet Toomer had not sat in judgment upon Karintha and Fern, who were also creatures of instinct. Jean Toomer, one suspects, expected such behavior from them—they were the Southern blacks, the children of nature. But Avey had been reared in Washington. She had been educated and had had opportunities to improve her economic position. She was of his group. She should have been able to rise above the animal.

Finally, pervading the stories is the sense that human beings need assistance from a superhuman power, a god or a messiah, which will affirm, console, sustain, and guide. Some protagonists in the South, living close to nature, dimly sense and vaguely follow the god of nature, who seems to affirm the actions of Karintha, offer the consolation of Jesus of the pines to Becky, and shelter Fern in a mystic experience. Even in the South, however, the religious power fails to provide what is needed. Becky, a Catholic, must confront the destructive god of the locomotive. Fern's Semitic character cannot flourish. Louisa prays helplessly to a "red nigger moon." Layman offers delusions. Father John mumbles incoherently. And messiahs vanish: Lewis retreats to the North and Barlo retreats into lusts of the flesh. Hope is even dimmer in the North for the urbanized, who cannot turn to religion, cannot even sense it. Southern-born Dan Moore, a would-be messiah, is a madman among the people of the North. There was, Toomer felt, a need for a new kind of salvation; and, as he completed his work on the materials of *Cane*, he became increasingly concerned with helping people discover that new salvation.

In *Cane*, then, although Toomer said that he wrote about a waning way of life, he also wrote unconsciously of the death of an artist. Jean Toomer the lyricist was dying; Jean Toomer the philosopher, psychologist, reformer was coming into being.

In 1923 Jean Toomer's path was bright. Editors were publishing his work and asking for more. But the publication of *Cane* in September marked the end of a road. Afterwards Toomer never again wrote about people who can be identified as Afro-Americans. After *Cane* Jean Toomer disclaimed identification with the Negro race.

In "Earth Being" Toomer wrote that *Cane*, to him, was "a swan song. It was a song of an end [of a certain way of life for Negroes]. And why no one has seen and felt that, why people have expected me to write a second and a third and fourth book like 'Cane' is one of the queer misunderstandings of my life." Although plausible, Toomer's explanation seems mere rationalizing when judged against other facts. In June of 1922 he had written to John McClure:

> As near as I can tell, there are seven race bloods within this body of mine. French, Dutch, Welsh, Negro, German, Jewish, and Indian. . . . One half of my family is definitely white, the other, definitely colored. For my own part, I have lived equally amid the two groups. And, I alone, as far as I know, have striven for a spiritual fusion analogous to the fact of racial intermingling. . . . Viewed from the world of race distinctions, I take the color of whatever group I at the time am sojourning in. As I become known, I shall doubt-

less be classed as a Negro. I shall neither fight nor re-
sent it. There will be more truth than they know in
what they say, for my writing takes much of its worth
from that source.[50]

A month later, in the same letter in which he an-
nounced that he had exhausted the *Cane* material, he
implied an intention to continue to write about Afro-
Americans. While discussing his plan to accompany
Waldo Frank to the South to gather atmosphere for
Frank's *Holiday*, Toomer explained:

> Your letter, together with a bit of analysis on my part,
> have convinced me that the impulse which sprang
> from Sparta, Georgia last fall has just about fulfilled
> and spent itself. My book, whether it matures next
> month or next year, will place a period. A fresh, and I
> hope a deeper start will come from our coming ven-
> ture.[51]

In August, in a letter to *The Liberator*, after explaining his mixed ancestry, he continued:

> Within the last two or three years, however, my grow-
> ing need for artistic expression has pulled me deeper
> and deeper into the Negro group. And as my powers
> of receptivity increased, I found myself loving it in a
> way that I could never love the other. It has stimulated
> and fertilized everything of worth that I have done.[52]

Even if Toomer merely wanted to write a polite letter to
the West Indian editor of a magazine for an Afro-American market, he was not required to offer this explanation.
Furthermore, Toomer's correspondence reveals him to be
forthright and candid rather than tactful. Indeed, Toomer's letter to Sherwood Anderson in December reem-
phasizes his identification with Afro-Americans.[53]

As late as March 1923, Toomer was proposing to

Liveright a second volume of stories to be published after *Cane*, a volume based on the communistic influences on Afro-Americans in Washington:

> This upward heaving [of the black and brown world] is to be symbolic of the world of proletariat upheaval. And it is likewise to be symbolic of the subconscious penetration of the conscious mind.[54]

In midsummer, however, in answer to Boni and Liveright's proposal to publicize *Cane* as the product of a Negro writer, he protested, "If my relationship with you is to be what I'd like it to be, I must insist that you never use such a word, such a thought again." [55] Within five years, in "The Crock of Problems," he explained that he did not want to be labeled either Negro or white because identification with either group would prevent his fulfilling a complete relationship with the other. By 1930 he had disassociated himself from the Negro race. In that year he refused to permit his work to be included in James Weldon Johnson's *Book of American Negro Poetry*; he complained that a delusion about his ancestry persuaded editors not to publish his works; [56] and he remonstrated against the references to him as a Negro in the *New Freeman*.[57] Two years later he achieved the ultimate denial when he alleged, "Though I am interested in and deeply value the Negro, I am not a Negro." [58]

In his first autobiography, he blamed two people for the confusion about his racial identity: Waldo Frank and his grandfather. Toomer argued that Waldo Frank first had mistakenly presumed that he was Negro. Then, incapable of understanding Toomer's explanation of his attitudes about race, Frank had compounded the error by identifying him as Negro in the introduction to *Cane*. Toomer explained that he had protested but had tolerated the error because he believed that no serious injury could result from such a trivial mistake.[59] The second man responsible for the error was P. B. S. Pinchback, who had professed being a Negro. Pinchback, Toomer argued, was sufficiently shrewd to have claimed Negro ancestry merely to win political support during Reconstruction.[60]

There are many possible explanations for Toomer's denials of African ancestry. One is that he actually may have begun to believe that Pinchback had lied about his race. A second is that Toomer may have believed that the time was convenient for such a denial; Pinchback's death in 1922 eliminated the man who best could repudiate the allegations. Furthermore, Toomer had been welcomed into the literary circle of Waldo Frank, Gorham Munson, Kenneth Burke, Hart Crane, Matthew Josephson, Malcolm Cowley, Paul Rosenfeld, Van Wyck Brooks, and Robert Littell. Toomer may have believed that he could participate in such a group more freely if he were not identified as Negro. (In "Natalie Mann," Nathan Merilh, Toomer's self-portrait, is accused of passing as white when he goes to New York.[61]) This third explanation seems improbable, however: Frank and Munson, who introduced him to the others, knew him as Negro.

A fourth possibility is that he decided to follow the advice of Waldo Frank. In an undated letter responding to Toomer's protest that Sherwood Anderson wanted to restrict him to writing as a Negro, Frank advised:

> the day you write as a Negro, or as an American, or as anything but a human part of life, your work will lose a dimension. How typical that is of most recognition: the effort immediately to limit you, to put you in a cubby hole and stick a label underneath. . . . the important thing which has at length released you to the creating of literature is that you do not write as a Negro . . . that you take your race or your races

naturally, as a white man takes his. The few talented writers among the Negroes have been ruined because they could not forget. . . . the world would not let them forget.[62]

Toomer had expressed a similar idea much earlier. In 1922 when he considered establishing a literary magazine for Afro-American writers, Toomer feared that

it will be some years before Negro contributors will rise to the level and abundance of filling a genuine literary magazine. The great majority of them are so entangled in "progress" that when one does emerge, he invariably bears the earmarks of the emasculated social machine.[63]

But this explanation of Toomer's change of heart seems to be refuted by the fact that, as late as March of 1923, he proposed to continue to write about Negro subjects.

Another possibility is that Toomer had sincerely reached a point at which he wished to avoid identification with any group. In A Fiction and Some Facts, he wrote,

As for being a Negro, this of course, I am not—neither biologically nor socially. . . . In biological fact I am, as are all Americans, a member of a new people that is forming in this country. If we call this people the Americans, then biologically and racially I am an American. . . . As long as I have been conscious of the issues involved, I have never identified myself with any single racial or social group.

In a diary written about 1930, he confided,

My desire to be dominant, to have the freedom and power of at least the social world, will not allow of my being colored, for the colored world is dominated and segregated. I must live, first, as an individual.

Is it, as Paul Rosenfeld thought, that I am to interpret the white to the black, the black to the white? Or is it that I am to decrystallize these divisions and make possible the widespread consciousness of the American race?

Certainly one can believe Toomer's sincerity in such statements as those quoted. If he assumed "Negro" to be synonymous with "African" or to identify a member of the "Negroid" race, he was correct that biologically he was not Negro: no scientific description of "a Negro" would have pictured Jean Toomer adequately. It is even more important, however, to notice that he is not merely denying that he is black; he is also denying that he is white. Instead of identifying himself as black or white, Negro or Caucasian, he insists that he is a member of a new race—"the American"—which has evolved from the older races. The idea was not new for Toomer. As early as 1922 in "Natalie Mann," he had emphasized the fusion of the African with the European; in his early autobiographical notes for editors he had identified several nations in his ancestry. Nor was this concept of an American race merely a passing fancy: Toomer adumbrated it and expanded it in poetry and in nonfiction throughout his remaining years.

What is surprising in this matter of racial identification, therefore, is not Toomer's development of a concept which was philosophically viable even if it could not be realized in a society which for three hundred years had emphasized the separation of the white from the nonwhite rather than the fusion of the groups. Instead, what is surprising is that during the summer of 1923 Toomer suddenly protested vehemently against a racial identification which a few months earlier he had accepted casually as a matter of slight importance. One looks for a significant occurrence between March and

July. And one finds it. In June, finally accepting Waldo
Frank's long-standing invitation to come to Darien, Con-
necticut, Toomer met and fell in love with Margaret
Naumberg, Frank's wife.

Love was not new to Toomer. Tall, fair-skinned, sufficiently handsome to be compared with Adolph Menjou,
well-developed physically through exercises practiced re-
ligiously since childhood, a graceful dancer, a hypnotic
conversationalist, Toomer had discovered his attractiveness to women before he was twenty. Moreover, love was
important to the young man who had experienced too
little of it from his family. In an autobiography he wrote,

> All my life I had had one main quest; and in so far as
> I have moved by inner impulse, my turns, returns,
> lapses and crossings have followed love.

In a diary of 1930, he wrote:

> To search life mainly in experience. When one is in
> this face [phase] if he is of the type able to turn rich
> experience intensively with a woman, he will seek
> and find and search with a woman who can energize
> him to search life with her and in experience. Books,
> art, study—these will be subordinate if not completely
> laid aside.

Margaret Naumberg was not the first and would not be
the last. Dorothy in grade school, Vic in high school,
Phyllis when he was a freshman at Wisconsin, Eleanor
in Chicago, a girl in Ossining, Beth, Emily, Mae (he had
planned to marry despite the eleven-year difference in
their ages), and most recently, Kitty: he had believed
that he loved them. But Margaret was different. He had
assumed the role of intellectual and spiritual guide for
the others, just as Nathan Merilh tried to help Natalie
Mann. Margaret, however, guided him. More than
twenty years later, he recalled that when he met her, he

"felt the whole world revolve." [64] She awakened him to a new consciousness: "My birth . . . came from my experiences with M. Naumberg." She helped him work out his philosophy concerning the functioning of mind, emotion, and body; perhaps she introduced him to the teachings of Gurdjieff. "My vision," he wrote, "was the one and only important thing in the world to me—that, and Margaret."

It is interesting to speculate whether his meeting Margaret Naumberg in the summer of 1923 precipitated his abrupt shift of racial attitude. Actually, however, it is not important to know what caused him to change; what matters is that Jean Toomer's artistic stature diminished after he repudiated his African ancestry and rejected Afro-American subjects.

Even if she was responsible for his change of attitude, Margaret Naumberg should not be singled out as the villain to blame for Toomer's decline as an artist. In addition to Toomer himself, there is a third—the philosopher George Gurdjieff. In Gurdjieff, whom Toomer met during Gurdjieff's visit to America in the fall of 1923, Toomer found the father-hero whom he had sought since childhood. Gurdjieff's influence was profound. In 1930, before he withdrew from Gurdjieff's group, Toomer wrote, "With certain notable exceptions, every one of my main ideas has a Gurdjieff idea as its parent." In 1936, after disillusionment with Gurdjieff's moral shortcomings had caused him to separate from the group, Toomer continued to accredit the source of his inspiration:

> I am not sure that I have a soul . . . but if I have then Gurdjieff has penetrated the shell and written upon the kernel indelibly. [65]

Unfortunately, Toomer's worship of Gurdjieff marred his writing. Seeking to be a philosophical Gurdjieff, he ceased being Jean Toomer, a lyric impressionist. Years later, Gorham Munson lamented Toomer's error:

I have been hoping in the past that you would see for yourself that Gurdjieff's "sublime egotism" at moments is unapproachable by us when we write, and that you would see the difference between his vernacular raciness and what I must call your lapses into a wooden colloquialism.[66]

The years 1924 and 1925 were sterile for Jean Toomer the artist. In 1923 Kenneth Macgowan refused to produce "Kabnis." Although he praised the dialogue and characters, he felt that the work lacked dramatic design.[67]

In July of 1924, Toomer studied at Gurdjieff's institute in Fontainebleau, France. When he returned to New York, he assumed the role of disciple. In *The Big Sea*, Langston Hughes has satirized Toomer's failure uptown: He "returned to Harlem, having achieved awareness, to import his precepts to the literati." [68] Wallace Thurman, Dorothy Peterson, Aaron Douglass, Nella Larsen, and others became neophytes. But the Gurdjieff method required time for inner observation and silent concentration. If the working Harlemites took the time they needed, they lost their jobs and could not pay Toomer for his teaching. "So—Jean Toomer . . . went downtown to sow the seeds of Gurdjieff in less dark and poverty-stricken fields." [69]

Toomer remained in New York through early winter. Then, in 1925, sponsored by Mabel Dodge Luhan, he carried the Gurdjieff gospel to New Mexico.

During the following summer, he retreated to Maine, where he tried to complete the manuscript of a new book, "Values and Fictions," a philosophical summary of his attitudes about race, art, literature, and self-realization. He disposed of the matter of race somewhat abruptly by pointing out that most people were too ignorant to talk about race. Scientists, anthropologists, and other scholars can identify racial distinctions, he argued; but few others are knowledgeable about these actual distinctions. Therefore, when the average person speaks of "race," he is merely explaining his prejudices.

It is significant and ominous to note Toomer's new attitudes about literature. In 1922 he had emphasized its artistic value:

> I do conceive of literature as an art. It is innate in me. The other sort of stuff I cannot write, as easy as many of my friends think it should be for me. . . . I am violated to think of literature as nothing more than a vicarious experience of what one should be strong enough to wring from the social life.[70]

A week later, he added, "A feeling for rhythm is basically essential to artistic expression." [71] In "Values and Fictions," however, he emphasized the moral rather than the artistic value. Literature, he insisted, should help the reader achieve consciousness. Literary critics have frequently debated whether the central purpose of a writer is to entertain, to create art, or to instruct. Toomer had never favored a focus on the entertainment value. Now, however, he proposed to elevate instruction above art. A year earlier, while predicting success for Toomer, John McClure had advised him to emphasize his talent for lyricism.[72] Others apparently agreed with this estimate, for publishers repeatedly rejected "Values and Fictions." The first was Horace Liveright who, in 1925, was still waiting for a new book from Toomer.

During 1925–26 Toomer's only creative publication was "Easter," a symbolic sketch.[73] By the end of 1925, Toomer, back in New York, was artistically sterile. In the summer of 1926 he studied again at Fontainebleau; in the winter he lived in Chicago.

His literary interests rekindled in 1927, however. During the year he completed three long works: "The Sacred Factory," "The Gallonwerps," and "The Crock of Problems."

"The Sacred Factory," which Toomer described as a

modern morality play, is an imaginative Expressionistic
drama written at a time at which the experimental movement in American drama—led by Eugene O'Neill, John
Howard Lawson, Elmer Rice, and John Dos Passos—
was eliciting increasing attention from the Broadway reviewers. Toomer envisaged, for his play, a compartmen-
talized set in which pillars divide the stage into three
chambers without separating walls. The domed central
chamber has a triangular rear opening which reveals
the light of a single star. The chambers on the two sides
suggest the world of the middle class and the world of the
workers.

The drama begins with a pantomine of the life history
of workers.[74] Stiffly, the Man and the Woman dance in a
circle. The Man leaves the circle in order to go to his
job; he returns; they eat, sleep, arise, and repeat the
monotonous routine of the lives of the working classes.
Children join the circle, then leave. The Man dies; the
grief-stricken Woman enters the central chamber of the
stage.

In the chamber of the middle class, John, Mary, and
Helen awaken. John, a scientist, is the husband of Mary
and the father of Helen. The first lines of the play focus
on their conflict. When Mary describes earth romantically as a little speck of dust on a great vast elephant
full of stars, a chorus laughs, and John interrupts to
begin a quarrel. John represents the atheistic, intellectual, rational attitude of modern man, who has failed to
achieve his spiritual potentiality. Mary personifies the
faith, emotion, and antirationality which characterize
modern, unrealized woman. The two individuals cannot
blend their personalities into a single force. They quarrel
until Being enters; then Helen, the daughter, enters the
central chamber.

The play has several weaknesses. It lacks action and
dramatic design. The ending is vague. Nevertheless,

since less artistic expressionistic plays were produced during the twenties, it is surprising that Toomer's was not.

"The Gallonwerps" is a drama, but the form and tone are different from those of "The Sacred Factory." Obviously influenced by George Bernard Shaw, Toomer attempted a satiric drama to teach audiences the need for self-realization. Wistwold Gallonwerp, of Billboa (Chicago) in Baaleria (land of Baal, god of wealth), is an idealistic pedant who wants a chance to explain his ideas about Man's salvation to America's leaders. Knowing that America's social and cultural leaders will ignore an invitation from her unknown husband, Wimepime Gallonwerp, who is famous for her beauty, has enlisted the assistance of mysterious Prince Klondike of Oldrope (Europe), reputed to be the wealthiest and one of the wisest men in the world. The prince is famed as a master of "diking," the art of manipulating events so skillfully that the diker is applauded by the very individuals whose interests suffer from the dike.

The prince (Toomer in a Mephistophelian mask) uses the occasion to perform a mission and a dike. While helping Wimepime "realize" herself, he steals Little Gasstar from Elginbora, the nurse. Metaphorically, the Ego releases the Id from the inhibiting Superego.

Despite occasionally incisive satire, the play fails. Most of the characters are lifeless allegorical representations of social types, whom Toomer first proposed to present as gigantic marionettes surrounding three real people—the lecturer (Wistwold), the woman (Wimepime), and the reformer (Klondike). A few puppets are admirable: a professor, a naturalist, a cultured world traveler, a heroic leader of men, and a metaphysician. The others are shallow-minded and imitative: a cloying, blank-minded spinster; a helpful Puritan; a gossip; a social leader; an effeminate artist; a social climber; a nouveau riche; and an "authority" (on everything). Moreover, the plot depends too heavily upon Toomer's psychological concepts. Without a previously acquired understanding of the concepts, a spectator would be bewildered. Without significant plot, the drama relies upon humor for entertainment. But too often Toomer's satire becomes crude and spiritless burlesque.

Although Toomer's friends generally acclaimed his works, even they protested against "The Gallonwerps." Fred Leighton, a businessman, suggested that Toomer needed to shorten it and add more comedy.[75] More knowledgeable about literature, Gorham Munson was better able to specify the weaknesses of the play. He wrote:

> I cannot think of it as successful. . . . I applaud this production for its aim and design, but I fear that you have not paid enough attention to the strange psychology of the reader. You must assume indifference on his part and compel him to be your slave. (This is the famous pleasure of art.)[76]

In "The Crock of Problems," his third work in 1927, Toomer proposed a solution for interracial antagonisms. Racial attitudes, he wrote, represent a complex problem because they are directed by both external and internal forces. Prejudice about race is not innate; it is learned from others. Hence, prejudice itself arises from a source outside the individual. The extent and the duration of this prejudice, however, are affected not merely by various external situations—such as the nature and quality of the association with members of other races—but also by the nature of one's psyche. Thus, "the race problem" is a term used to cover a class of complex maladjustments located in living people and mixed with many other things—sex, sexual competition, jealousy, fear, etc. To illustrate the complexity, Toomer told of a white father who dissuaded his son from marrying an Afro-American girl by arguing that blacks are mentally and physically inferior because of inherited organic deficiencies and that they are morally inferior because they are the descendants of Negro women who have produced illegitimate children. The problem of the father is not merely his acceptance of fictions about blacks but also his fear of what people will say (social psychology) and his identification with his son (personal psychology). Toomer insisted that such a complex issue can be solved. First, men must be taught to live in such a way that they will escape psychic malfunctioning. Second, a new race must be evolved—one which is not white, not black, but American.

In the book, Toomer redefined his attitude about his ancestry. So many different bloods were mixed in him that he could not say that he was either "colored" or "white." In popular usage, he continued, those terms do not designate race; they indicate an attitude toward life. A "colored" person is one who is cut off from life with white people. Therefore, Toomer could not define himself as "colored," for he associated freely with white people. On the other hand, a "white" person (with Negro blood) is one who passes for white by avoiding contact with black people; but Toomer had not avoided them. Furthermore, any label would prevent having "on a larger scale such exchanges with both groups as I want." Colored people suspect white people of patronizing them or of seeking self-expression among them. White people suspect colored people of overly aggressive attempts to effect social contacts and to gain equality. Hence, "contacts between white and colored people tend to be automatically reduced to discussion of race and race relations, and nothing else." He assured both groups that, as a human being, he was a member of each group, but that he refused to "belong" to either one if such attachment excluded him from the other. He offered, finally, to contribute "the meaning and value" of his life to creating a new society, "a great Internation of all peoples," governed by the natural merit of those who possess the greatest intelligence (scientific and philosophic knowledge), conscience (religious and artistic force), and ability (creative force and power).

As he had proved in his earlier attempts to crusade for socialism at the height of the Communist scare, Toomer was singularly out of touch with the temper of his society. In 1927 the Ku Klux Klan, having infiltrated the North, enjoyed its greatest strength since Reconstruction days. Meanwhile many Americans still peeked under their beds for black-bearded Bolshevists carrying bombs. Such an America was not prepared to listen to ideas about an international brotherhood or a mixture of races. It is not surprising that publishers rejected "The Crock of Problems" even more quickly than they rejected "The Sacred Factory" and "The Gallonwerps."

Despite the continuing rejections of his longer works, 1928 brought literary success which encouraged him to believe that he had found the path again. Marianne Moore accepted "White Arrow," a poem, for *Dial*, a magazine which Toomer had wooed unsuccessfully in the early twenties; and Kenneth Burke published "Mr. Costyve Duditch" in the same magazine.

"Mr. Costyve Duditch" is the story of a man who might have been included in the gathering at the Gallonwerps. Unable to achieve satisfactory, enduring relationships because of his conscious sense of inferiority and his unsuspected lack of imagination, Costyve compensates by impressing himself upon people. For example, he tips extravagantly so that servants at hotels will remember him. He proposes to write three books: one describing the influence of travel on personality, a second recounting the love affairs of a great man, and a third explaining the creative processes in life and in art. Temperamentally, he is incapable of writing any of the three.

The plot is thin. Mr. Duditch has just returned to his home in Chicago for the usual brief respite from travels in Spain, Constantinople, Persia, and China. He rises at nine A.M. to follow his accustomed routine of tasting the atmosphere of the business district of the city in which he finds himself. When he clumsily breaks a glass bowl in the Marshall Field Department Store, he becomes so embarrassed that he decides to leave Chicago three hours earlier than he had intended. He is staying that long only because he has promised to attend an afternoon tea. At the tea he is delighted when talk about his travels makes him the center of attention; but his insensitive discussion of death shocks the socialites into awareness of its inevitability. Knowing that he has clumsily broken something again, Duditch hurries away to catch his train, "rushing and active with fuss and to-do, surrounded by things and people though he was, his spirit hugged itself in loneliness and felt goaded by a thousand shattered hopes."

The merit of the story is not the plot, which is awkwardly handled through clumsy shifts of point of view. The merit is the sympathetic, though somewhat satiric, delineation of Duditch, a lonely and unimaginative wanderer.

"Duditch" is characteristic of Toomer's post-*Cane* style, but "Winter on Earth," published in the *Second American Caravan*, recalls the lyricism of *Cane* itself. Paul Rosenfeld praised the excellence of the idea of blending the style and inspiration of *Cane* with the philosophy apparent in his new efforts.[77] After an introductory philosophic attempt to identify the earth as a microcosm in a vast universe, "Winter on Earth" gains strength from three scenes: a lyric description of snow and cold sealing the city in a wintry blanket; a poignant picture of two tramps who seek shelter from the cold; and perceptive narration of an incident in which a young man seduces his friend's wife. The final section of "Winter on Earth" powerfully evokes the dreariness and barrenness of the winter-buried land.

Despite his reviving fortunes in literature, Toomer was unhappy and confused. The death of his grandmother in autumn deprived him of the last link with an actual family. Although he continued to be identified romantically with women, his disbelief in the permanence of passionate love caused him to withdraw from long-standing engagements.[78] There is more than a little of Toomer to be seen in the lonely, people-surrounded Costyve Duditch.

As consolation for his lack of permanent personal relationships and for the failure of his longer manuscripts, Toomer clung to his "mission." In 1927 he had boasted,

> What I have done has won me literary recognition and position. And if I wished to devote the time and energy to it, I could now be one of the strongest forces in American literature. . . . But I have in mind becoming something much greater than a literary force, and for this "something" I am deliberately sacrificing certain things in the present.[79]

The "something much greater" was his mission as a spiritual reformer, a role which he had assumed frequently throughout his earlier life. Both at the University of Chicago in 1916 and at the East Side Settlement House in New York in 1918, he had lectured to and advised youths. His success with his friend Harry Kennedy in Washington in 1918 had persuaded him that he possessed the talent to reform people. His early romances had been characterized by efforts to develop the latent nobility of the young women. Following his summer study at Fontainebleau in 1924 and 1925, he had become leader of the Gurdjieff group in Chicago. His work did more than satisfy his desire to improve people; it provided intoxicating admiration. Letters from his female disciples proclaim their worship. Even a male follower, Jeremy Lane, predicted that Toomer might become a new Messiah. Such adulation would have delighted anyone's ego, but it was particularly heady for a man desperately striving to emulate the imagined prominence of his father and the actual prominence of his grandfather. His sense of commitment to a mission did not end until 1932, when, disillusioned by Gurdjieff's charges of mishandling funds and by Gurdjieff's scandalous behavior during a trip to America, Toomer drifted away from the man even though he still clung to the philosophy.

Meanwhile, Toomer continued to write. He hoped to use literature to reform people. He hoped to support himself on royalties. Most of all, however, he needed to be able to express his ideas to an audience.

In 1929 he was optimistic about his future as a writer:

> During the past years since *Cane*, I have written much, but only now are my things nearing a form suitable for publication. Again my writing is appearing in the magazines, and what appears there is but a foresign of what I have in progress.[80]

Principally he was preparing four works: "York Beach," "Winter on Earth," *Essentials*, and "Transatlantic."

In "York Beach," he offered a revision of "Istil," the first five chapters of which appeared in the third *American Caravan*. Based on his trip to York Beach, Maine, with Paul Rosenfeld in 1928, the work describes the experiences of Nathan Antrum (Toomer) and Bruce Rolam (Rosenfeld). As usual, the plot focuses on an unrealized female. Weakly written, "York Beach" smothers a synopsis of a novel under the blanket of a philosophical treatise.

"Winter on Earth," a collection of stories, is a more successful literary effort. In addition to "Winter on Earth," and "Mr. Costyve Duditch," Toomer included "Love on a Train," "Lump" (also entitled "Clinic"), and "Drackman." Each of the last three is a story in which the action reveals the psychological confusion of the protagonist. In "Love on a Train," a temporarily successful flirtation teaches Dr. Meron Coville that he must learn to experience each moment of life vividly without regret for its impermanence. In "Lump," Jonathan Curtis, accustomed to position and influence, experiences an ego-wounding loss of identity when he is forced to visit a clinic for a minor operation. In "Drackman," a wealthy businessman, Daniel C. Drackman, is suddenly attacked by egomania, which causes him to view the entire world of New York as an extension of himself. Toomer's talent transformed these case studies into art, but he failed to secure a publisher.

Essentials is a collection of aphorisms, through which Toomer sought to define his philosophical and psychological doctrines.

"Transatlantic," written in seventeen days, narrates a shipboard romance between an isolated, self-exiled man and a spiritually undeveloped woman. Undoubtedly the book was motivated by the fact that publishers had been encouraging him to write a novel ever since he had written *Cane*. He still had nothing to tell in long form, however, except the often attempted story of Jean Toomer and Woman.

Toomer's optimism about his resurging fortunes was ill-founded. His works were rejected. The most disappointing was the rejection of *Essentials*, which five different publishers turned down in 1929 and 1930. Publishers' readers liked it but believed either that the

Depression was not a time at which to publish a collection of aphorisms or that Toomer needed first to reintroduce himself to the public by writing a novel. Ogden Nash, with Doubleday, expressed his admiration but doubted that the book would sell commercially.[81] A reader for Coward-McCann also feared the times:

> A great deal of it I like very much and so do the other people in the office, but in these times it seems impossible to undertake the publication of such a book.

A reader for Macmillan promised to reconsider *Essentials* and "Winter on Earth" after Toomer wrote a novel.

The Depression and his years away from the reading public were affecting his fortunes, but Toomer rationalized his failure by arguing that publishers, considering him Negro, expected another *Cane*. Consequently he redoubled his efforts to disassociate himself from Afro-Americans and their literature. Meanwhile, faith in the merit of *Essentials* persuaded him to publish privately a limited edition of one hundred copies in 1931.

Feverishly he wrote, but publishers rejected calmly. He wrote "Bride of Air," a collection of poems intended as a companion volume for *Essentials*, and he revised "The Gallonwerps" into a wordy and ineffectual novel. A. A. Knopf rejected both. Despite his failure to sell *Essentials*, he wrote "Remember and Return," a longer collection of aphorisms;[82] Putnam's rejected it. He had also written "The Spiritualization of America," or "A New Force for America": "A prose analysis of the main psychological factions and tendencies—race problems, human problems, mechanization and sensualization of life—which make Americans hate life and from which they can be saved only by a new religion." He had "Winter on Earth" ready for publication, had completed "Blue Meridian," and was working on an autobiography, "Earth Being," and on a revision of "Transatlantic."

Despite the frenzied activity, his only publication was "Brown River, Smile," a portion of "Blue Meridian," a poem which he had been composing for ten years. A paean to the spiritual union of races in America, "Blue Meridian" was cursed by Toomer's ill luck. J. Middleton Murry accepted the poem for *Adelphi*. But when the magazine changed its format, the poem was judged too long; consequently, only 125 lines were published.

In the summer of 1931 Toomer established a cottage in Portage, Wisconsin, where for two months he conducted an experiment in spiritual growth among a group of male and female followers of Gurdjieff. Toomer believed that he succeeded in helping his followers "realize" themselves. He was especially pleased with the assistance he gave to Margery Latimer, a talented writer who, Toomer felt, used her literary ability to shield herself from a world which she could not accept. Having known her earlier in the Gurdjieff group, Toomer had been a confidante about her intimacies with Zona Gale and male admirers. In 1931, he fell in love, and on October 20 married her.

1932 began auspiciously. The happily married Toomer took his wife to Carmel, California—he, to work on "Portage Potential," a too candid description of his triumph in developing human souls; she, to await the child whose birth she hoped would fulfill her life. The year ended in misery.

Troubles began when one of the participants in the Portage experiment was sued for divorce by his wife, who, alleging that he had committed adultery, referred to his activities at Portage. The scandal was intensified by Toomer's naïve responses to interviewers. Although Toomer would not have offended Gurdjieffan exponents of free and full development of mind, soul, and body, he shocked many non-Gurdjieffan Americans recuperating from what they considered to be the moral anarchy of the twenties. Moreover, the writers for national magazines reminded their readers that Toomer, a Negro, was married to a Caucasian.

To explain how their innocent love created a national scandal, Toomer wrote "Caromb"—the title a combination of Carmel and Somber. By July he had completed the novel, which, despite passages of lyric beauty, reveals the artistic defects which might be expected in a hastily written apologia by a man who did not fully understand why there was any scandal.

Before the scandal subsided, additional disaster struck. In August, his wife died in childbirth, leaving him with an infant daughter, legal complications about royalty rights for Margery's publications, and the financial problems harassing millions of people during the most serious economic depression in America's history.

By the end of the year, Toomer had rededicated himself to literature. When Harrison Smith of Smith and Haas Publishers rejected "Caromb" as an "interesting book but a little too formless to make a really first rate novel," Toomer responded,

> For some years I have been struggling with the auto-biography-fiction problem. To date, I have not reached a satisfactory solution. . . .
>
> Heretofore I have held, unconsciously, conflicting attitudes as to details. One part of me has said. "You must convey and incorporate them into the body of your work, else your work will lack body and it will lack relatedness to the very people for whom you are writing. . . ." Another part of me has said, "Detail is uninteresting, and why should anyone bother to put in a book that which our days—even our nights—are already sufficiently full of. . . ." Perhaps a marriage of these attitudes would enable me to produce a book . . . sufficiently projected, sufficiently unusual and essential.
>
> . . . I have repeatedly told myself that my inten-

tions could not be realized in the short time—one, two, to three months—I allowed for each book. Why then have I done as I have done? Partly because I had set myself the task (and I could not have done otherwise) of building a world in literature, and this world, to me . . . was so vast that I felt that only by rapid intensive work could I ever in my lifetime even approach a fulfillment of my aim. (Now, I see, I had my eye too much on the large structure I had in mind, not enough on the specific book. . . .) Partly because, in general, I couldn't help it. The pressure of circumstance—or something—compelled me to forge ahead and do the best I could, with the hope that this best would be in some degree worthwhile, and that it might win a place for the book, and somewhat arrange conditions so that I could then write a better book, and a better one, and so on. . . . What some people call "leisure for creation," I have never known. . . . Now, however, I realize I must have time for ripening and for workmanship.[83]

Characteristically, however, within ninety days Toomer set a schedule which allowed only two months for his projected book.

Jean Toomer may have considered 1933 a year of new beginnings aften ten years of fruitlessness, ten years of wandering. Regrettably, it was a literary end, which he ironically predicted in a letter to Harrison Smith accompanying the final draft of the long delayed "Eight Day World," the revision of "Transatlantic": "Despite the defects I am satisfied that it is my best work thus far, and I have a feeling that my future is linked with what happens to it." When Smith rejected the work, Toomer for the first time in his correspondence with publishers disclosed his desperation. Explaining the importance of publishing the book, he pleaded:

I have an enormous material and force—so much that if I were to have no further experiences, still would I have enough to write about for the rest of my life. In fact, I have already . . . in my mind no less than seven books planned. . . . We cannot demand of *Eight Day World* the aesthetic success which I will gradually achieve. . . . In fine, in relation to my future writing, the publication of this book means everything to me. I've got to know that the materials and the forms of this book are in the world, available to, and known by some number of readers.

Between 1924 and 1933 I went on a far journey into strange lands of experience—only this year have I come back, so to speak, to earth—and I've come back a different person from the person of 1923—and it is this relatively new person who is now *just beginning* to write. . . . And this new person is doing [sic] to put into literature things that haven't been there before. He is going to do this, not because of any desire to be original or strange, but because he has to, because this is the only way in which he can express himself and convey his material.[84]

Harrison Smith justifiably refused to publish the book. Toomer regarded "Eight Day World" as "a revelation of the psyche of a single man or woman,"[85] an explanation of the meaning of this terrestial and cosmic journey. He felt that for once he had expressed all the details. He was correct only that the book represented a new Toomer, with all of the flaws and few of the virtues of the old. The lyricist of *Cane* or even "Caromb" had perished. The sensitive delineator of enigmatic personalities had dessicated. The flippant, too conscious satirist of "The Gallonwerps" was gone. What remained was a smooth writer telling a tedious story about uninteresting people. In revising "Transatlantic," Toomer lengthened it, split the male and female protagonists, and added sex. These changes did not help. The male protagonist is still Jean Toomer—magnetic to and magnetized by women, philosophical, searching for identity and for relationships. The female protagonist is Woman, bewildered by her new independence and needing to grow spiritually and intellectually. The male protagonists seek women with the frenzy of a secretary trying on hats during a lunch hour. Unbelievable characters indulge in incredible seductions and assaults. As a first novel, it would be deplorable. As an effort by Jean Toomer, it is tragic.

"Eight Day World" begins during a farewell party for Harold "Hod" Lorrimer, a "handsome dark devil with a mass of romantic curly black hair, blue eyes spaced far apart, a bold face, a strong regular nose, lips full, sensuous, with the touch of cruelty a man should have." Modeled on one aspect of the character of Toomer—as he wanted to be or as he was—Hod is an egocentric materialist who believes that a man needs only sex and love. At the party, Hod's most recent mistress, Vera, regains control of her emotions after Hod's rejection and decides to reward herself with a trip abroad on the same boat on which Hod is sailing. After quarreling with Sid Case, who objected to Hod's mistreatment of Vera, Hod invites Sid and Sid's wife Betty to accompany him abroad. Also voyaging on *The Burgundy* are Hugh Langley (Toomer's other self), an idealistic but skeptical man, who rigidly controls his emotions, Andra Feala, and Barbara, Hod's wife. Hugh is immediately attracted to Vera, Barbara, and a young girl; but characteristically he restrains his emotions. Even though he and Barbara are mutually attracted physically and emotionally, they seek to maintain their relationship on a level of friendship.

After Hod and Hugh reach an agreement in a scene reminiscent of the Ahab-Starbuck discourse in "The Symphony" in *Moby Dick*, Hod goes to the third-class section, where he wordlessly seduces a tourist after three dances with her. By evening of the following day, the tourists, aroused by Jim Phillips, a Communist "agitator," are expressing their protests against Hod's casual seduction.

The next morning Hod visits Andra Feala, who has spent the night with her twenty-five-year-old lover, Andy Sherman, who can free the femininity repressed in her since childhood. Hod, interested in Andra, maneuvers Andy into a situation in which he is humiliated by the rebuffs of Hod's friends. Having spent much of the day talking with female passengers, especially Emily Gilroy, a young "liberated" woman, Hugh that evening dances soulfully with Barbara, toward whom he has begun to assume the attitude of protector. After the dance, Hugh hears from Andy Sherman that Hod wants to talk with him. He soon learns, however, that the message was merely a means of separating him from Barbara, who, returning to her cabin, is accosted by Andy, who seems ready to attack her but who collapses, recovers, and leaves. Back in the salon, Hugh considers his desire to make love with Andra, but he leaves her to Hod, who spends the night in her cabin.

The next morning, when Andy cannot be located, Hod blames himself for the supposed suicide. Meanwhile, Barbara blames herself for restraining her expression of gratitude for Hugh's assistance. After another day of conversation, the passengers again divert themselves in the salon. Hod has turned his attention to yet another woman, and Andy has been discovered in a lifeboat. After a sustained attempt to reeducate Edith Gilroy, Hugh dances with Vera, persuades her that he does not love Barbara, and makes love to her.

On the final evening of the voyage, the ball is interrupted by the tourists from third class who, still angry, crash the party. After Hod has started a fight with him,

Hugh buys a farewell gift for Barbara, who, having read Hugh's notes, has learned of his interest in her. Within sight of England, Jim Phillips makes a final assault, but again fails to disrupt the first-class passengers. Wishing to help her because she is lonely and uninformed, Hugh talks with Barbara; but at the end of the journey, he leaves with Vera. Having learned that Andra is interested in him, Hugh considers seeing her in Paris. After the ship has docked, the passengers separate, and the eight day world has ended.

Although the tangled summary does not reveal the psychological and philosophical dimensions of the work, it does suggest the quality of the story.

Toomer refused to accept the pronouncement of the end of his career as a writer. But when creativity depends upon a beginning which no one will accept, no future remains. He could not return to the style and thought of *Cane.* He refused to recognize his major limitations— inability to develop a dramatic plot, inability to write about himself effectively, and refusal to write about any- one else. He could not free his art from his dogma. To understand his work, one needed to comprehend and to believe his philosophy that the only meaningful life is a continuous growth toward Being, a process requiring the separate and total development of mind, soul, and body. Beyond that philosophy, nothing existed. Toomer could sketch, lyrically or realistically, the people whom he knew. His talent was perhaps restricted in range, but it approached genius within its limits. But the engraver wanted to paint murals and could not.

The remainder of his life records a repetition of suc- cessive literary failures and few successes. *Adelphi* in England published "The Spiritualization of America" as "A New Force for Co-operation," but Max Lieber, his

American agent, refused to try to sell the essay. Viking rejected "Eight Day World," "The Letters of Margery Latimer," and "Blue Meridian and Other Poems." In 1935, after considerable delay, *The Dubuque Dial* published "Of a Certain November," a story. Having joined American Dramatists in 1934, Toomer toyed in 1935 and 1936 with the idea of a trilogy of lecture-dramas viewing people as objects of satire, of purgation, and of objective pity. He never completed it.

Although he published two Socratic dialogues, "Make Good" and "Good and Bad Artists," on the Literary Page of the *New Mexico Sentinel*, the following years added to the rejections of "Remember and Return" and of "Talks with Peter," a record of conversations about matters. In 1939 and 1940 he sought spiritual identity and growth in the Pacific and in India. Failing, he turned to the Friends Society, for which he began publishing philosophical essays and reviews of religious works, reviews characterized by a tolerance noticeably absent from the strident critiques which he had written during the early twenties.

Having abandoned fiction, in the forties he tried to publish "From Exile into Being," an explanation of a mystic experience in which, after feeling himself detached from his body, he was able to integrate his body and his mind in such a way that he could see the true relationship of man to the universe.[86] This was rejected, by publishers, as was "The Second River," a more detailed explanation of the experience and of his philosophy. In the mid-forties he expected his friend Denver Lindley to publish his autobiography, "Earth Being," later entitled "Incredible Journey." But Lindley, moving from Appleton to Holt, evaded the issue and let others reject the book. A new volume of poems, "The Wayward and the Seeking," was rejected with praise by Longmans, Green and Company.

During the late forties he lectured. In 1948 Toomer wrote to a chaplain who would introduce him in a speaking engagement at Vassar. Toomer identified himself as the chairman of the Executive Committee of Ministry and Counsel of the Philadelphia Yearly Meeting of Friends. His activities included meeting with Friends and conducting seminars for them, addressing forums and poetry societies, and writing articles, reviews, and poetry (most frequently published in the *Friends Intelligencer*).[87]

His mission still summoned him as late as 1948. "Since 1924, I have made effort to promote in myself and in others, catharsis-development as a means of growing up to God through transformation and new birth." However, complaining of tightness in his mind (as he had in 1923) and of difficulty sleeping, Toomer underwent Jungian psychoanalysis to discover the blockage in his life. In 1949 he explained to a friend that there had been discrepancy between what he was and what he could do. He had written, but not one book had really connected. He had lectured without financial return. He had taught and advised people but could not charge them. Consequently, he had lacked money and, since his marriage to Marjorie Content in 1934, had depended on her for most of his support. "There has been in me," he wrote, "for many years, some obstruction, some twist, some blockage, so that what is in me has not been able to come out freely and in ways that would connect on all planes, with the life of our time—and with the needs of myself and those dear to me. . . . Some inner handicap has prevented me from living up to what I have reason to expect of myself and to what others have reason to expect of me.[88] Even his faith in his books had waned:

It is possible that those and other of my writings will be "discovered" one of these days, and be published, and do all I had hoped they would do. It is also possible and even probable that none of them have really come off, that they are not worth publishing because I was not able to put the real stuff into them.[89]

At the age of twelve, physically debilitated and humiliated because he no longer was respected as the leader of his gang, Eugene Pinchback withdrew from his friends, climbed a post, and contemptuously observed his former playmates from his isolated seat. In *Cane* he wrote of isolated individuals seeking not to belong but to be. After *Cane*, Toomer, self-exiled from all races and from the material and style which served him best, named the isolated protagonists Nathan or Hugh or Hod, but they were all self-portraits of Jean Toomer, exile. In his last years, Toomer, exiled to a nursing home, reassumed the seat of "Pinchy" on the post. He died on March 30, 1967. But he had written his own epitaph sixteen years earlier:

> I have found that what is effective for me at one time . . . does not necessarily carry through to all other times and periods. So then, the searching begins anew.
>
> Perhaps, Sandy, our lot on this earth is to seek and to search. Now and again we find just enough to enable us to carry on. I now doubt that any of us will completely find and be found in this life.[90]

2

Countee Cullen
The Lost Ariel

The poet laureate of the Harlem Renaissance was Countee Cullen, the most popular Afro-American writer since Paul Laurence Dunbar, who had died almost twenty years before Cullen published his first book. Precociously Cullen produced three books of original poems before he lived twenty-six years, but he never attained the literary heights promised by his first works. Diverse reasons have been offered to explain the diminishing of his powers. Stephen Bronz described it as another "of the subtle contradictions surrounding an apparently simple figure." [1] Some critics have implied that he had nothing significant to write about after he rejected Afro-American subjects and themes. Others have reasoned that public school teaching consumed the time and energy which he might have devoted to the creation of poetry. Cullen himself attributed his decline to indolence. [2] These explanations, however, fail to consider the desire which Cullen phrased prophetically while his reputation and his productivity were at the zenith:

> I hope that when I have sung my rounds
> Of song, I shall have strength to slay
> The wish to chirp on any grounds,
> Content that silence hold her sway. [3]

A significant writer—even a lyric poet—must perceive some truth, some reality which he wishes to reveal. It is the quality of this vision which elevates his song from the transitory to the memorable. In his earliest poems,[4] Cullen sought such truth in a presumed affinity with Africa. He wanted to believe that impulses of his African heritage surged past his censoring consciousness and forced him to repudiate the white gods of Western Civilization. Cullen's Africa, however, was a utopia in which to escape from the harsh actualities of America, and the heritage a myth on which he hoped to erect a new faith to comfort himself in a world seemingly dedicated to furthering the interests of white men.

It is debatable whether Cullen fully believed in subliminal racial impulses or in racial memories stored in a Collective Unconscious. If he did believe, he may have lost some confidence when critics cynically observed that his racial memories had recorded inexact descriptions of Africa. Certainly, however, the actual Africa was no lodestone. Although he traveled abroad during eleven summers, Cullen never visited "the scenes his father loved."

As the African impulse waned, Cullen knelt before the altar of love, but there also false gods demanded sacrifices he would not offer. Like a wanderer disconsolate after a worldwide search, Cullen turned back to Christ. But he still could not rely upon the white god who governed the Methodist Church in which he had been reared; he could not believe a white god capable of comprehending the depths of a black man's suffering. Therefore, he fashioned for himself a black Christ with "dark, despairing features." This image, however, furnished scant comfort; Cullen knew that his own creation could not correct mankind's transgressions. Without faith, without vision, Cullen, whom Saunders Redding has compared with Shakespeare's ethereal Ariel, lost his power to sing and soar above the fleshly Calibans. He turned to fiction, to prose, to drama, to other men's visions; and his production slowed. Finally, Ariel sank to rest in a kingdom of childhood, to sing of Christopher Cat and other animals more able and more majestic than the human kind.

Although there is some doubt about his place of birth and his parentage, the biographical facts about Cullen are relatively clear. He was born on May 30, 1903. Although his second wife and some of his friends have insisted that he was actually born either in Baltimore or in Louisville, Kentucky, Countee Cullen claimed New York City, where he certainly lived after he was nine years old. Separated from his mother in early childhood, he lived with Mrs. Porter, who was possibly his grandmother,[5] but he sought companionship from Frederick Cullen, the minister of Salem Methodist Church, who adopted him after Mrs. Porter died in 1918.

In Dewitt Clinton High School Cullen distinguished himself scholastically by maintaining an average of 92 and by earning a Regent's Scholarship. He demonstrated other talents. He won the Douglas Fairbanks Oratorical Contest, edited the Clinton *News*, and in 1921 served as associate editor of *The Magpie*, in which he published "Rendezvous with Life," a poem which won first prize in a city-wide poetry contest sponsored by the Empire Federation of Women's Clubs.

He continued to write poetry while an undergraduate at New York University, where he matriculated in 1922. In 1923 and 1924, his poetry received honorable mention in the nationwide Bynner Undergraduate Poetry Contest. Finally, in 1925, his "Poems" were unanimously selected for first prize. By the time he graduated, Phi Beta Kappa, in 1925, he had won additional prizes for poetry from *Palms*, *Poetry*, *Crisis*, and *Opportunity*, and he had published *Color*, a collection of his poems.

After earning a Master of Arts degree in English from Harvard University in 1926, he accepted a position as an

assistant editor of *Opportunity, A Journal of Negro Life,*
for which he wrote a monthly column, "The Dark
Tower." In 1927 two new volumes of his poetry—*Copper
Sun* (1927) and *The Ballad of the Brown Girl* (1927)—
were published, as was *Caroling Dusk* (1927), an anthology of Afro-American poets, which he edited. In
1928 he was honored with the first Harmon prize
awarded by the National Association for the Advancement of Colored People for "distinguished achievement
in literature by a Negro," and he received a Guggenheim fellowship.

He spent the following two years in Europe, where he
wrote *The Black Christ and Other Poems* (1929).
Shortly before he left for Europe, he married W. E. B.
DuBois' daughter, Yolande, whom he had known for
several years. After a summer's honeymoon in Paris, his
wife returned to her teaching position in Baltimore
while Cullen remained abroad. In 1930 she sued for divorce and obtained it.

After he returned to the United States in 1930, Cullen
flirted with the Communist Party, which he later repudiated in favor of Franklin D. Roosevelt's progressive program, and he published *One Way to Heaven* (1932) and
Medea (1935). Having declined two invitations to teach
in Negro colleges in the South,[6] in 1934 he accepted a
position as teacher of English and French at Frederick
Douglass Junior High School in New York City.

In 1940 he married Ida Mae Roberson, with whom
he lived until his death in 1946. During his last years he
published *The Lost Zoo* (1940) and *My Lives and How
I Lost Them by Christopher Cat* (1942). At the time of
his death, he was editing a collection of his poems, published posthumously as *On These I Stand* (1947).

From the beginning in *Color* (1925) to the end of his
poetic career in *Medea* (1935), Cullen was a lyricist, best
when writing subjectively and most effective when his

feelings derived from subjects sufficiently universal to encourage a reader's interest and, possibly, identification.

Cullen first achieved significant recognition for "The Ballad of the Brown Girl," which was named for honorable mention in the Witter Bynner Poetry Contest of 1923. Cullen, who did not always remember sources and influences accurately, stated that the poem was based on a ballad which he had heard in Kentucky in 1915.

The story tells of Lord Thomas, who, encouraged by his mercenary mother, marries the wealthy Brown Girl rather than Fair London, whom he loves. When Fair London insults the Brown Girl at the wedding feast, Lord Thomas refuses to avenge his wife. After the Brown Girl exacts her own vengeance by killing Fair London, Lord Thomas strangles her with her own hair, curses his mother's false advice and kills himself. The three lovers are buried in a single grave: Lord Thomas and Fair London side by side, and the Brown Girl at their feet.

In the poem Cullen did not master language and imagery. He retained such archaic expressions as "I wot," "clipt," and "thicked" (thickened). He exaggerated images. Perhaps the most grotesque appears in the narration of the murder: "He pulled it [her hair] till she swooned for pain/And spat a crimson lake."

Despite such extravagances, the poem earned accolades. Witter Bynner named it first choice among the entries for his contest; George Lyman Kittredge, Professor of English at Harvard University, judged it the finest modern rendition of an old ballad which he had ever read. Cullen sustained the ballad rhythm effectively, narrated suspensefully, and subtly diverted attention from the major theme of love versus money to the secondary theme of the white persons' cruelty to the Brown Girl. The implications are unmistakable. Fair London, the "lily maid," is the "pride of all the South." Although the Brown Girl is a descendant of kings, Fair London refuses to drink with her. Moreover, the Brown Girl is buried in the traditional slave woman's resting place—at the foot of the bed of her mistress—"in the land where the grass is blue," an image certain to evoke thoughts of Kentucky in the minds of American readers.

In the following year, 1924, Cullen was disappointed to earn only honorable mention for "Spirit Birth" in the Bynner Poetry Contest. Continuing his interest in racial themes, Cullen, in the poem, credited his African heritage for giving him the will to live. Despondent because he recognizes that America destroys any Negro who asserts his manhood, the poet prays for death. A series of mystic visions then reveals to him the universality of the struggle for existence. In the first he sees the efforts of plants and animals to survive: "all was struggle, gasping breath, and fight." Worms dig tunnels in search of light. Seeds blossom, climb, die, and, as seeds, blossom again. The newly flowering rose mocks his cowardice. But the success of nature's creatures fails to mitigate his despair. A second vision shows the eternal struggle

> Of beast with beast, of man with man, in strife
> For love of what my heart despised . . .
> And no thing died that did not give
> A testimony that it longed to live.

But he responds only, " 'let them fight; they *can* whose flesh is fair.' " Even the vision of warring angels fails to motivate him to want to live. One vision remains, " '*this failing, then I give/You leave to die; no further need to live.*' " The poet listens to the music of Africa. He sees the chained slaves, and senses even among those "a harmony of faith in man/A knowledge all would end as it began." Fortified by awareness that the dark-skinned

people of the world continue to struggle against op-
pression, he casts doubt aside:

> "Lord, not for what I saw in flesh or bone
> Of fairer men; not raised on faith alone;
> Lord, I will live persuaded by mine own."

Although Laurence Stallings judged it to be the best
poem published in the *American Mercury* in 1924, "The
Shroud of Color" (Cullen's new title for "Spirit Birth")
is unconvincingly suspended between a personal cry and
an allegorized sermon.

Ironically, in the poem, Cullen prophesied his future
psychological agonies. At twenty he refused to base his
reason for living on either God or white men. In all of
nature only the black man could inspire him. But what
if he lost this one faith? Then nothing would remain for
him except the desire to die.

In 1925 Harper and Brothers published *Color,* which
is heavily weighted with poems oriented to racial consciousness. Twenty-three poems, approximately one-third
of the book, focus on Afro-Americans. Included are some
of his best-known poems: "Yet Do I Marvel," "A Brown
Girl Dead," "Incident," "Saturday's Child," "The
Shroud of Color," and "Heritage."

The despair of "The Shroud of Color" is underscored
in the couplet which ends his sonnet, "Yet Do I Marvel": "Yet do I marvel at this curious thing:/To make a
poet black, and bid him sing." Although he accepts even
the seemingly paradoxical blindness, death, tortures, and
frustrations of life, he, nevertheless, is amazed that God
would expect unrestrained artistic expression from one
restricted and oppressed because of the color of his skin.

In the other poems, however, Cullen did not despair.
Instead he praised the courage and the beauty of Afro-
Americans, exulted in their glory, exuded sympathy for
them, and chanted his faith in his heritage. In "To My

Fairer Brethren," for example, he boasted of achievements by blacks, who must defeat their white brothers three times before the victory is considered anything other than an accident.

In *Color*, Cullen perpetuated the unprovable idea that African heritage endows a black man with passion and rhythm superior to a white man's. In "A Song of Praise" he did not merely commend the beauty of the dark-skinned girl; he even demeaned the blonde, whose blood is "thin and colder." In "Atlantic City Waiter" he described the graceful movements of a black waiter: "Ten thousand years on jungle clues/Alone shaped feet like these."

A popular stereotype of the Afro-American in twentieth century American literature is that of a child of nature, whose uninhibited behavior is directed by unrestrainable passion, innate rhythm, and an inherent talent for music. Although the discordant singing and clumsy dancing of some blacks should stir the suspicion that some of these generic impulses have been dammed during their four-centuries flow, the myths persist as part of the noble-savage image which during the twenties was transferred from the South-Seas native to the Afro-American. Whereas some blacks have exploited the myth consciously, others, like Cullen, have succumbed to it. For instance, he knew that he could not sing well; but, to justify his belief in his inherited musical talent, he described his poetry as "the way of my giving out what music is within me. Perhaps I was impelled toward the lyrical pattern, when I began to write, because a destiny took pity on my musical poverty." [7] The myth, it must be admitted, occasionally helped his reputation, for even when his sense of rhythm faltered badly in *Copper Sun*, his next book, one critic, nevertheless, reminded readers that Cullen "has rhythm, precise and unfailing, in his blood." [8]

Cullen's atavistic urge is most apparent in "Heritage," the lyric cry of a civilized mind which cannot silence the memories of Africa that thrill the blood, of a heart which responds to rain and which, prostrate before the Christian altar, yearns for a black god who might comprehend suffering as no white god can. Despite the atavism, "Heritage," which surpasses "The Shroud of Color" in imagery and diction, is the most successful lyric poem Cullen ever wrote.

Only one-third of *Color* is concerned with Afro-Americans. The other two-thirds include a section of epitaphs, a section of love poems, and a section of poems on miscellaneous subjects. Skillfully chiseled cameos, the epitaphs reveal Cullen's ability to compress thought and image. He pays tribute to a grandmother who believes in resurrection and to a cynic who judges death to be the end. He mocks the virgins who hoard their love until death, and satirizes a lady who expects to be attended by Negro servants, even in heaven. He derides those who seek eternity in earthly philosophies, which inevitably end in the grave. He honors distinguished men—John Keats, Paul Laurence Dunbar, Joseph Conrad. Anarchists, evolutionists, atheists, pessimists, philosophers, unsuccessful sinners, fools, skeptics, fatalists, wantons, heroes, and saints: all earn appropriate four-line summations. But he empathizes most with wantons and fools, and he praises most highly the people who wisely have seized every treasurable pleasure from life's brief course.

In many of the miscellaneous poems, Cullen revealed significant elements of his thought. There is an abundance of love poems on the "carpe-diem" theme. A reminder of Cullen's habitual sympathy for outcasts echoes from his speculation that Jesus commanded Judas to betray Him so that His mission would be fulfilled. In four poems, Cullen repeated the death wish of "The Shroud of Color." Although the yearning for death is not unexpected in poetry written by sensitive youths, the juxta-position of this theme and the "carpe-diem" theme of other poems suggests that his occasional challenge to life was merely a mood which could evanesce into despair. His brash boast to battle the world in "Harsh World That Lashest Me" ends with a reminder that he can leave whenever he wishes. In "Requiescam," he wrote an appropriate epitaph for himself:

> I am for sleeping and forgetting
> All that has gone before;
> I am for lying still and letting
> Who will beat at my door;
> I would my life's cold sun were setting
> To rise for me no more.

Although they were his first, the poems of *Color* are representative of the talent which he maintained throughout his writing. His poetry differs from that of Paul Laurence Dunbar or Jean Toomer. More specific and more thoughtful than Dunbar in imagery but less impressionistic than Toomer, he concentrated upon conventional rhythms, pretty images, and provocative thought.

Cullen did not experiment with rhyme and meter; his needs were satisfied by iambics in four- or five-foot lines, ballad meter, rhymed couplets, and blank verse. Generally, he handled metrics competently; however, he sometimes faltered. In one poem he reduced "forest" to a word of one syllable. In "Two Who Crossed a Line (She Crosses)" he wrote, "Only the silence in her face/ Said seats were dear in the sun."

He pictured more precisely than Dunbar did, but he lacked the sensuousness of John Keats or even Toomer. In carefully chosen phrases, he communicated emotions through the mind and the eye rather than through the senses or the blood. He succeeded in such lines as, "for

a fitful space let my head lie/Happily on your passion's
frigid breast;" [9] and his description of life in Africa—"a
land of scarlet suns/And brooding winds, before the
hurricane/Bore down upon us;" [10]—or such an effective
phrase as, "My heart is pagan mad." [11] Frequently, he
stimulated response by shocking conceits:

> Who knows
> But Dives found a matchless fragrance fled
> When Lazarus no longer shocked his nose? [12]

Perhaps the major weakness is that a reader becomes too
conscious of the craftsman manipulating deceptively
simple phrases, of the artist who occasionally delighted
in irony and deliberate ambiguity.

At this stage of his work, Cullen, like Toomer at the
time of *Cane*, linked his artistry to his racial consciousness. In March 1926, he said, "In spite of myself, however, I find that I am activated by a strong sense of race
consciousness. This grows upon me, I find, as I grow
older, and although I struggle against it, it colors my
writing." [13] More than a year later, he reemphasized his
interest in Afro-Americans as a subject: "Somehow or
other, I find my poetry of itself treating of the Negro, of
his joys and his sorrows, mostly of the latter and of the
heights and depths of emotion which I feel as a Negro." [14]
But, after 1927, Cullen argued with intensifying vehe-
mence that Negro poets should not be compelled to write
about their race.

When Frank Mott advised Negro authors to write
about Negro subjects, Cullen, with uncharacteristic passion, denied that they ought to be interested in any particular subject. Arguing that Browning and Shakespeare
had written about nations and times other than their
own, he demanded the same liberty for Afro-American
writers.[15] As Cullen would not discount the ability of
white writers to depict blacks perceptively,[16] so he would

not deny a black writer the opportunity for excursioning: "Let the test be how much of a pleasant day he himself had had, and how much he has been able to impart to us."[17] As if unable to forget the injustice of restricting artists to one subject or one mode of expression, he returned to the thesis later in "The Dark Tower" by attacking the white people who assume that Afro-Americans can sing only spirituals.[18]

One month later he responded more temperately to Alain Locke's introduction to *Four Negro Poets*, in which Cullen was included: "We have serious doubts that Negro poets feel themselves more strongly obligated to their race than to their own degree of personal talent."[19] Later, he wrote of himself,

> he has said with a reiteration sickening to some of his friends, that he wishes any merit that may be in his work to flow from it solely as the expression of a poet —with no racial consideration to bolster it up.[20]

Two years later, he raged,

> Then call me traitor if you must,
> Shout treason and default!
> Say I betray a sacred trust. . . .
> I'll bear your censure as your praise
> For never shall the clan
> Confine my singing to its ways
> Beyond the ways of men.[21]

Black critics were not the only ones forcing burdens upon Cullen. He felt the pressure everywhere. In 1929 he remonstrated with a white author:

> Must we, willy-nilly, be forced into writing of nothing but the old atavistic urges, the more savage and none too beautiful aspects of our lives? May we not chant a hymn to the Sun God if we will, create a bit of phan-

tasy in which not a spiritual or blues appears, write a tract defending Christianity though its practitioners aid us so little in our argument; in short do, write, create what we will, our only concern being that we do it well and with all the power in us.[22]

Much of Cullen's protest arose from his fear that an author restricted to writing about his race would be stereotyped and isolated from the main body of American literature. "Just now," he wrote in 1927, "I can really imagine nothing quite so emblazoned with interest as being a Negro. It is to be *a la mode* and who would be the fashion should remember that in a slip-shod world to be the vogue is also to be peculiar and apart." [23]

Furthermore, even though he respected crusading poets, he did not choose to use poetry as a weapon in such crusades. For him, poetry was the most beautiful expression of the human mind. In 1926, while debating the poetic quality of Langston Hughes's jazz verse, he wrote,

> I wonder if jazz poems really belong to that dignified company, that select and austere circle of high literary expression which we call poetry.[24]

Two years later he defined poetry:

> Good poetry is lofty thought beautifully expressed. . . . Poetry should not be too intellectual. It should deal more, I think, with the emotions. The highest type of poem is that which warmly stirs the emotions, which awakens a responsive chord in the human heart. Poetry, like music, depends upon feeling rather than intellect, although there should, of course, be enough in a poem to satisfy the mind, too.[25]

By that time, however, he was defining poetry partially to defend himself against critics who had been disappointed by his second volume of poetry, *Copper Sun*

(1927), even though it earned him the first Harmon prize awarded for distinguished achievement by a Negro in literature. Beulah Reimherr has charged that Cullen's error was to disregard Mark Van Doren's advice by publishing a second book too quickly. Others have claimed that he weakened his poetry by turning from racial themes; only seven of the fifty-eight poems constitute the "Color" section of *Copper Sun*.

Although both of these charges may have merit, a third must be considered. Countee Cullen, poet, failed to respect the advice of Countee Cullen, literary critic, who condemned immature poets' failures to criticize their own poetry,[26] who praised Robert Browning's insistence that poets should not bare their hearts,[27] and who later defined poetry as "lofty thought."

Despite occasional flashes of brilliance which remind a reader of his potential for greatness, Cullen failed to distinguish himself in *Copper Sun*. He reexamined racial themes which he had explored previously in *Color*. Too frequently, he wrote phrases and images which echo artistically superior passages from Percy Shelley, John Donne, Edna St. Vincent Millay, and A. E. Housman. He included several love poems which are so personal or so petty that they cannot evoke empathy from sensitive readers. He wasted paradoxes, conceits, and sparkling images on trivial subjects and themes.

Nevertheless, despite Cullen's limitations, *Copper Sun* is not a poor book. Some poems are quite good. "From the Dark Tower" is one of his most respected poems despite its ambiguous ending. "Lovers of the Earth: Fair Warning" and "More than a Fool's Song" present provocative thought about the values of life and about social outcasts. If *Copper Sun* had appeared before *Color*, it would have persuaded readers to anticipate masterful lyrics by the author in his more mature years. Published after *Color*, however, it disappointed readers because it evidenced no significant improvement in metrics, imagery, or thought. In fact, Cullen seemed to be weakening rather than improving.

In June 1928, Cullen left America and his bride in order to begin his Parisian tour of duty as a Guggenheim Fellow. He had proposed to write a series of narrative poems and a libretto for a musical comedy. Instead, he produced "The Black Christ" and forty-five generally undistinguished brief lyrics on occasional subjects and about love.

The pervasive sorrow and acerbity reflect Cullen's bleak moods during a marriage which apparently ended as soon as it began. In the first twenty-seven poems, the "Varia" section of *The Black Christ and Other Poems* (1929), one-third contain images of sorrow, and one-third present images of death. The second section, "Interlude," is a series of lyrics expressing bitterness, disillusionment, and sorrow about the loss of love. The major poem of "Color," the third section, is "The Black Christ," the narrative of the lynching of a Southern black man who became a friend of a white woman.

The Black Christ is an unpleasant book. The imagery and the language evoke admiration. But the subject matter produces embarrassment comparable to that experienced when, visiting during a domestic quarrel, one is compelled to listen to the self-pitying despair of someone who cannot, who will not, be consoled. Yet, only a year earlier, Countee Cullen, literary critic, had admonished poets not to bare their hearts.

Amid the self-pitying cries and childishly petulant defiances are some well-conceived poems and vivid images. Their major weakness is one which Cullen implied in "Self-Criticism":

> Shall I go all my bright days singing,
> (A little pale, a trifle wan)
>
> . . . .
>
> Shall I never feel and meet the urge

To bugle out beyond my sense
That the fittest song of earth is a dirge
And only fools trust Providence?
Than this better the reed never turned flute
Better than this no song.

The best poem in the book is the title poem, "The Black Christ," the story of a miracle which converted the black narrator from atheism to a belief that Christ will save the world. The narrator once lived in the South with his mother and his brother Jim, an arrogant, handsome youth whose continual questioning of the ways of life and God had persuaded the narrator to deny God's existence. One day in spring, Jim met a young white woman in the country. Briefly they shared the day's beauty until they were interrupted by a white man who insulted them. Angered, Jim attacked the man, then ran home to hide from the lynchers who were certain to pursue. Soon, however, Jim emerged from the closet where he had been hiding. To the narrator, he seemed so strangely transformed that he illuminated the room. He let himself be dragged to the top of a hill, where he was hanged from a tree. While the narrator continued to mourn his brother and curse God, Jim again stepped from the closet. Then the narrator realized that Christ had substituted Himself for Jim and, once again, had sacrificed Himself to save mankind.

"The Black Christ" is an impressive failure. Cullen proved his ability to sustain lyric intensity throughout a long poem. He created images as effective as any others in his poetry, and he created persuasive, although somewhat stereotyped characters. Above all, he skillfully developed a somber mood through subtle contrasts: nature's springtime beauty is scarred by man's ugliness; the innocence of Jim's friendship with the girl is soiled by the lascivious inferences of the white man who sees them; skeptical, rebellious Jim contrasts with his mother, who suffers in the South but who refuses to leave her home.

Despite these achievements, Cullen failed both in conception and in execution. First, he carelessly contradicted his theme. Ostensibly, the theme is that each day Christ is killed by man's injustice and violence. Christ asks the narrator to dedicate himself to proving by love and charity that He has not died in vain:

> For no life should go to the tomb
> Unless from it a new life bloom,
> A greater faith, a clearer sight,
> A wiser groping for the light.[28]

Yet He sacrifices Himself to save a murderer. Although he was attacked physically as well as verbally, Jim did not allege that he killed in self-defense; instead, he said that he killed the white man because the man was destroying springtime's beauty. By sacrificing Himself, Christ, therefore, sanctions murder, which, He has said, destroys Him each time it is committed.

Furthermore, Cullen disregarded the necessary restrictions on literary uses of a Christ-figure, who can be used to personify suffering or to denounce the anti-Christian behavior of mankind, but cannot be employed effectively as a sacrificial victim. The reason is obvious. The emotional tension from a killing is determined by a reader's capability of empathizing. In the Passion Play, Christ evokes pity from people who think of him as a man who was born of woman, was reared among mortals, shared their agonies, was forced to carry a huge cross whose weight made him stumble, and died hanging from that cross. But, a Christ-figure in a twentieth-century situation inevitably assumes the stature of a god who has been reborn. Such an omnipotent being cannot evoke the requisite pity from readers, who, knowing that the god cannot die, await with pleasurable anticipation a new demonstration of Christ's power to transcend death. Consequently, the black Christ's act of replacing Jim in the lynching does not evoke pity; it merely becomes a *deus ex machina* for rescuing the protagonist.

Even if Cullen had perceived the dimensions of his theme, he might have failed because of faulty narrative technique. In order for the reader to experience the desired dramatic tension at the climactic incidents, he must recognize the Christ-figure while Jim's brother remains ignorant. But, because the brother tells the story, he alone can present the identifying clues. Thus, possessed of all the facts, the narrator seems obtuse when he fails to make the identification.

Cullen also revealed weaknesses in poetic techniques. By writing iambic tetrameter, he forced a sprightlier rhythm than seems appropriate for solemn incidents, and he frequently failed to sustain the metrical pattern. Furthermore, the movement is impeded by the end rhyme, and inverted or artificial phrasings evidence Cullen's willingness to sacrifice artistic expression to the demands of the rhyme scheme.

After *The Black Christ*, Cullen wrote no more poetry for six years. His next major publication, *One Way to Heaven* (1943), was a novel.

When Carl van Vechten's *Nigger Heaven* (1925) appeared, Cullen did not add his voice to those praising the novel. Mildly he questioned the authenticity of van Vechten's depiction of Afro-Americans in Harlem, where, he said, one can find "a clarified vision of the wit, the dauntless humor, the endless good nature and kindliness" [29] of the Negro. If he hesitated to castigate van Vechten, he did not restrain his fervor when he advised black writers to depict Afro-American life discreetly:

Let art portray things as they are, no matter what the consequences, no matter who is hurt, is a blind bit of philosophy. There are some things, some truths of Negro life and thought, of Negro inhibitions that all Negroes know, but take no pride in. To broadcast them to the world will but strengthen the bitterness of our enemies, and in some instances turn away the interest of our friends. . . . *Put forward your best foot.*[30]

When Cullen wrote his first novel, however, he ignored his critical prohibition. He told the story of Sam Lucas, a vagabond who preys upon gullible blacks by pretending to be converted to Christianity.[31] Lucas's game is simple and effective. Calculating the appropriate moment in a revival meeting, the one-armed Lucas strides to the front of the church, silently pulls a deck of cards and a razor from his pocket, hurls them to the floor, falls on his knees, and surrenders himself to God. Each time his performance is rewarded with meals, a few dollars, and the admiration of some woman. Before he is forced to take vows as a new convert, he moves to a new town to repeat the act.

After one such performance in Harlem, he meets Mattie Johnson. Attracted to her and somewhat tired of wandering, he courts and marries her. Soon frustrated by the stability of married life, however, he drifts into an affair, deserts Mattie, and takes up residence with another woman. Brought back to Mattie because he is dying of pneumonia, he deceives her one final time. Knowing that she wants to believe that God will save his soul, Lucas pretends to have seen the necessary signs.

One Way to Heaven is not an artistic triumph, but it is better than the average novel. As a first work, it is particularly promising.

Cullen created memorable characters and caricatures. Despite his deceitfulness, Sam Lucas is neither wicked nor contemptible. Indolent, indifferent to the Christian dogmas, Sam gambols gaily through life accepting charitable contributions of food and love where he finds them. Although he enjoys satisfying sensual appetites and delights in playing cards and dancing, he is neither a noble savage nor an amoral being. He elicits sympathy for his actions. Even his straying from his wife to another woman is reasonably motivated. Egotistical and restless, he flirts casually with Ellie May, with whom he works daily. When his wife becomes such a strict Methodist that she spends her evenings in church meetings, he turns to Ellie May to heal his wounded ego. When Mattie further humiliates him by praying for his soul at a church meeting, he goes to Ellie May. He returns to his wife when she becomes pregnant but leaves once again after she has lost his child. Lucas certainly is not an admirable figure, but he is credible. Seen through the eyes of Aunt Mandy, he is a typically sinful but charming male.

Cullen probably modeled Mattie Johnson after parishioners in his foster-father's church. She had been born in Alabama but had come to New York as a child to live with her aunt and uncle. Although she lives modestly, she has refused to join a church. Once she has been converted by Sam's pretended conversion, however, she quickly becomes a fanatic. Although she loves Sam, she cannot understand that Sam, needing assurance that he is her god, is jealous of her all-absorbing devotion to the Christian god.

The major flaw in the otherwise credible delineations of Sam and Mattie results from Cullen's melodramatic attempt to introduce excitement. Learning of Sam's affair, Mattie, armed with a hatchet, visits Ellie May. When Ellie May confesses, however, Mattie is so horrified that she drops the hatchet and runs home. That evening, Sam slashes their bed with a razor when he drunkenly tries to kill Mattie. That Mattie would consider murder is incredible; that she would arm herself with a hatchet is farcical. That Sam, even when drunk, would attack Mattie is equally incredible.

Cullen's most delightful characterization is Aunt Mandy. She practices Methodism scrupulously while in the church, but outside she uses charms to help the Christian god. Loving God and loving man, she is a companion to Sam and a raisonneur for the novel.

Cullen established a secondary setting in *One Way to Heaven* in the home of Constancia Brandon, self-appointed queen of the high society of Harlem. When he depicted this group, however, Cullen descended to caricature. Having been part of this group which was assured of artistic or financial success, he felt freer to laugh at them than at the struggling members of the lower classes. As Constancia says,

> "An irrefutable evidence of a sense of humor . . . is the ability to laugh at oneself, as well as at one's tormentors and defamers. If we haven't learned that in these three hundred years, we have made sorry progress." [32]

Unfortunately, because the educated, artistically talented people are ridiculed while the uneducated are delineated sympathetically, it appears that only the uneducated blacks are truly commendable.

Constancia Brandon, an intelligent, well-bred Negro from Boston, impresses society with her vocabulary and her parties. Insensitive to racial problems, she enjoys collecting people who will provide excitement and laughter for her soirées. Included among her menagerie are Lottie Smith, a blues singer; Mrs. De Peyster Johnson, a chauvinistic sponsor of Afro-American artists; Bradley Norris, a "New Negro" poet; Sarah Desverney, a librarian, who discounts the merit of any Negro author after Paul Dunbar and Charles Chesnutt; Donald Hewitt, a young Englishman who believes that Harlem's soirées are America's only resemblance to England's culture; Lady Hyacinth Brown, a housewife, and the Duchess of Uganda, an elocutionist, who have earned their titles as rewards for raising funds for the "Back to Africa" movement; and Stanley Bickford, a Nordic-looking architect, who spends much of his life explaining that, in America, he is considered a Negro.

By describing the interaction of this group with occasional white visitors to the gatherings, Cullen ridiculed several popular myths about Afro-Americans. Dr. Seth Calhoun of Alabama, author of *The Menace of the Negro to Our American Civilization,* gamely fulfills his obligation as guest lecturer by explaining to the politely attentive Afro-Americans that they are immoral and smell bad. Other targets of satire are a missionary, absurdly zealous to enlighten the heathen, and a gullible white man who readily accepts as authentic "Negro" costume whatever is worn at the soirées.

In dialogue which is sometimes less sparkling than one would expect from a poet writing a comedy of manners, Cullen ridiculed foreign audiences for lavishing praise upon mediocre black entertainers without realizing that more talented performers go unnoticed in the black-populated cabarets of Harlem. He satirized chauvinistic posturings by Afro-Americans, their failure to buy books written by others of their race, and their penchant for discussing and condemning books which they have not read. Occasionally Cullen also instructed white readers in interracial etiquette—the proper pronunciation of "Negro" and the offensiveness of using "your people" when talking with an Afro-American.

The soirée scenes in chapters 9 and 10 are perhaps the most entertaining in the book. Echoing, yet surpassing, van Vechten's *Nigger Heaven* and the satires of Wallace Thurman, they seem to be the work of a mild-mannered Sinclair Lewis reporting a gathering of Scott Fitzgerald's folk. Nevertheless, they constitute a structural defect in the novel because they seem unrelated to the story of Mattie and Sam. Although Cullen labored to effect a connection based upon Constancia's interest in her maid's romance, it is improbable that such a status-conscious Negro as Constancia would condescend to involve herself in the personal affairs of her black servant. Instead, she would be anxious to emphasize the difference and the distance between herself and her maid. Furthermore, because the scenes are witty, they glitter so distractingly that they divert the reader from the commonplace though poignant story of Mattie and Sam.

In 1935 Cullen published *The Medea and Some Poems.* The subtitle to "The Medea," "A New Version," suggests more changes than are apparent. When Cullen's version is compared with Murray's prose translation of Euripides' play,[33] there seem to be few significant differences in structure and characterization. Cullen departed from Euripides, however, in some interesting and revealing ways. In addition to limiting the number and the length of the choral odes—a concession to the tastes of a modern audience, he eliminated Euripides' pronouncements against divorce and his pleas for greater freedom for women. Cullen added imagery reflecting lust and greed for money, and he emphasized the alienation of Medea, an African woman who has betrayed her family for the love of an ambitious white opportunist.

The language vacillates between eloquence and colloquial stammering. Written in the idiom of twentieth-century America, the dialogue reads more smoothly than do most translations from the Greek. Yet Cullen too often sank into bathos in hackneyed colloquialisms and folk proverbs.

It is startling and distressing that King Creon, at a moment of tension, should exclaim, "Forewarned is forearmed," or "I'm not one for beating about the bush," or

"Charity begins at home," or "I'm one who 'says his say.' " At first, a reader presumes that Cullen consciously intended to deride the commonplace mentality of Creon, but Jason and Medea also speak tritely. Medea wishes that she and Jason had seen "eye to eye." In other instances, she says that there's "no bad blood between us" and that "he won't bite you." Because one wishes to adjudge Jason contemptible, one is less disturbed that he talks about his "cock o' the walk" enemies and says, "It's only natural for a women to go into a fit." The most shocking instance of bathos occurs when Jason confronts Medea after she has killed their children. After admitting with lyric simplicity, "I walk with grief," she continues: "I have paid off an old debt. We are quits now." The hackneyed colloquialisms seem appropriate only from the Messenger, who talks of "passing the word along," "patching up the quarrel," and "raising a hue and cry." Confusing banality with naturalness in diction, Cullen failed to write either a great poetic drama or dramatic poem, for either must be measured by the excellence of its language.

Cullen's emphasis upon Medea's African ancestry, however, is significant. Even though he continued to insist upon his right to select his own subjects and ridiculed the idea that Afro-Americans should return to Africa, Cullen re-created the situation of *The Ballad of the Brown Girl*: once again, an African woman is betrayed by a white man who has exploited her. As Medea proclaims herself a foreigner and castigates Jason for his willingness to abandon her while he seeks to ingratiate himself with the ruler of the land, a black reader suddenly perceives a new dimension in an old "Greek" story. Since it is doubtful that Cullen could have been unaware of this emphasis, which seems consciously developed, one must surmise that, no matter how much he insisted upon his right to be judged without reference to his race, Cullen could not erase from his mind the conviction that whites exploit and betray blacks.

In the twenty-four original poems included in the volume with "The Medea," Cullen showed his characteristic strengths and weaknesses. Not straining for complicated measures, he contented himself with short forms which he could compose quickly. Fifteen of the poems are Shakespearean sonnets, written chiefly on the theme of lost love. He maintained greater artistic detachment than he had in *The Black Christ*; but, regardless of the subject or the theme, the mood of the shorter poems is melancholy. Cullen described his mood best in "Sonnet": "I can only sing of what I know/ And all I know, or ever knew, is woe." He generally developed clear, appealing images, but he continued to publish carelessly finished poems. Insensitive to the crudities of his poetry, he concluded "Sleep" harshly:

> The bosom of the Night is shared
> By all her weary, stricken brood;
> And though the suck be short, 'tis good.

Blaming his poetic silence upon conflicting emotions, diverse friends, exotic settings, and indolence, Cullen implied his readiness to resume writing; but five more years passed in silence. When he published again, Cullen, happily married, was teaching English and French in a school in New York. After years of groping for faith, having lost his inspiration of Africa or first love, he retreated to the world of children and wrote books for that world.

In 1940 he published *The Lost Zoo*, a poetic account of the animals who, for human reasons, failed to embark on Noah's ark. Twelve-eyed Wake-up-World died from a heart attack caused by its overexertion while rushing about to awaken the other animals and hurry them aboard. Shy Squilililigee committed suicide because other animals incessantly mocked his name. Lazy Sleepamitemore, awake only twenty minutes per week, possibly slept through the flood. Possessed of instinct enabling them to locate any lost object, the Treasuretits stayed behind rather than expose themselves for forty days and forty nights to thoughtless animals who would abuse their talent. The two heads of the Double-headed Hoo-dinkus could not agree whether or not to go aboard. The Lapalakes were killed by swordfish because, phenome-nally thirsty, they threatened to drink all of the flood wa-ters. The Snake-That-Walked-upon-Its-Tail died because, excessively proud of his ability to walk on his tiny feet, he waited too long; he wanted to be the last to arrive so that all the other animals would admire his walking. The Ha-Ha-Ha foolishly disregarded Noah's warning. True to his characteristic love for outcasts, Cullen sympatheti-cally described Sammie Skunk's humiliation when big-oted animals petitioned Noah to exclude him from the group.

Cullen had given credit for coauthorship of *The Lost Zoo* to Christopher, a cat who recited stories which he had heard from his father. In his final book, Cullen, iden-tified merely as the amanuensis of Christopher, created a work possibly superior stylistically and structurally to his earlier novel. In Chris, Countee Cullen found a *per-sona* he could enjoy. Confident of the innate superiority of his species, as he informs the reader in his first words, Christopher suffers neither the frustration nor the inhi-bitions of his human scribe; consequently, he is relaxed and self-assured as he explains to his dull-witted human amanuensis how he lost his first eight lives.

Comparison of the two individuals emphasizes the fact that Cullen escaped into a character free from the re-strictions which had limited his own life. Christopher's father was a distinguished aristocrat: he traced his lineage to Noah's ark. His mother, though a commoner, provided all the love a growing kitten needs. With two brothers, three sisters, and a patient father determined to educate his kittens in proper "cateristics," Christopher, even during his first life, enjoyed family security which the human Cullen lacked until he was in his teens. Furthermore, not harassed by fellow cats urging him to be realistic or imagistic or chauvinistic or atavistic, or to write about this or that (Cullen did not dare to prescribe Chris's subjects), Chris was free to tell his story as he wished—sentimentally, suspensefully, digressively.

Reared with his brothers, and sisters—intellectual Claude, vain Claudia, lazy Carlos and Carole, and his twin Christobelle, young Chris learns the lessons essential to an educated cat: how to lap milk, how to wash, how to purr, and how to arch. He also learns that fathers sometimes err. Having been warned to avoid Rat, who is not a respectable companion for a cat, Chris meets Rufus the Ritten (if a young cat is a "kitten," then surely a young rat is a "ritten"; so Chris reasons with Humpty-Dumpty's logic). Similarly, Rufus's father has warned him against cats. Despite their prejudiced parents, Chris and Rufus become friends when they discover that they have identical habits and interests.

The work has all the elements essential to enjoyable fiction: comedy—the kittens must recite original poetry before company; pathos—the discovery that their father's cousin, Tom, is a disreputable adventurer, a discovery made too late to prevent Carlos and Carole from running away with him to join the circus; excitement—Chris's flight to the rooftops to escape a gigantic dog; tragedy—Christopher Senior's heroic death while rescuing a strange kitten from being crushed beneath a car, Mamma's death caused by her grief, and Christobelle's illness; farce—Chris's encounters with talkative Michael Monkey and with Towser Dog and Dobbin, retired country squires; and finally romance—Chris's unrequited love for the beautiful Royal Persian Scheherezade compensated by the discovery of true love and companionship with Mitzi, kitten of Mumtaz Tazmum, the beautiful, ill-fated cousin of Christopher Senior. In his ninth life, protected by devoted Mitzi, Christopher shares the home of a human being who also had found happiness in second love and who was nearing the end of his only life.

Even in these books for children, however, Cullen never persuades a reader that he has evaded consciousness of the discriminations against blacks. Christopher is a "catitarian" (and perhaps more sensitive than a "humanitarian"); consequently, in *The Lost Zoo*, he expresses chagrin that his ancestor had signed the petition against Sammie Skunk. Sammie's only fault was that, at times, he smelled bad; as Cullen reminded readers in *One Way to Heaven*, the allegedly offensive odor of blacks is a reason which bigots have used to justify the segregation of blacks from whites. Furthermore, in *My Lives and How I Lost Them*, Christopher Senior's explanation of why Chris must avoid rittens directly echoes bigots' pronouncements of the inferiority of black people.

In 1947 Harper and Brothers published *On These I Stand*, an anthology of Cullen's best poems, a book he had been preparing at the time of his death. Having six books of poetry from which to select and, consequently, not needing to include carelessly finished poems merely to piece out a book, Cullen developed an excellent volume. Reduced in number and mingled with many other poems on various subjects, even the painfully personal poems of *The Black Christ* appear to good advantage. Cullen included six poems never published before. One, "Dear Friends and Gentle Hearts," has been criticized as an example of Cullen's inability to evaluate his own work. As a lyric for a popular song, however, it exceeds the quality of most. Yet, except for "Karenge ya Marenge" [Do or Die], an impassioned plea for liberty for India, the six poems add little to Cullen's reputation.

Two books of poetry—*Color* and *On These I Stand*—one novel—*One Way to Heaven*—and a children's story —*My Lives and How I Lost Them*: these represent the contribution to American literature by Countee Cullen, poet laureate of the Harlem Renaissance, a prodigy who failed to fulfill the promise of his first book and who ended his productivity in a world of cats and children where, free from social and literary demands, he could evoke sentiment in a smoothly narrated tale. Ariel, in mask, finally found a base on which to rest.

3

Zora Neale Hurston
The Wandering Minstrel

Zora Neale Hurston was a wanderer. Born five months earlier than Countee Cullen, on January 7, 1903, in the all-black community of Eatonville, Florida, she experienced security and domesticity only during the first nine years of her life. For that brief period, she lived with her father, whom she loved and respected even when she was annoyed by his too complacent acceptance of the Southern social system, his indolent drifting with fortune's winds, his unministerial philandering, and his inability to understand her. Tolerated by her father, she was protected by her mother, who understood and encouraged her daughter's impudence, curiosity, and imagination. As Miss Hurston proclaimed in her autobiography, life in Eatonville was pleasant despite the limited financial income of the family.[1] Perhaps her family could not afford to buy the current fashions for her, but they provided clothing which protected her from the Florida climate and from immodesty. The family budget rarely afforded such delicacies as beef and apples; but the family garden provided ample stores of vegetables and fruit, and the poultry house assured a supply of meat and eggs. Snug in the family nest, Zora Neale Hurston was chilled only by her certainty that her father favored an older brother and worshipped an older sister.[2]

From 1912 until her death in 1960, Zora Neale Hurston wandered, rarely remaining in one locality for

longer than three years and often disappearing from
public view despite her prominence as the author of
four novels, two collections of tales, and an autobiography—more books than any other female Afro-American
had written. After her mother's death and her father's
remarriage thrust her from the nest in 1912, she fluttered
among relatives until, at the age of fourteen, she decided
to support herself. Hiring herself into a series of jobs as
maid and waitress, she migrated as far north as Baltimore, where she completed her secondary education at
Morgan Academy, which later, as Morgan State College,
awarded her a Litt.D. After Morgan, she enrolled at
Howard University in Washington, where she worked as
a manicurist while attending school. A scholarship assisted her to transfer to Barnard College, where she
earned a bachelor's degree. Subsequently she served as
secretary to novelist Fannie Hurst,[3] studied anthropology
under Dr. Franz Boas at Columbia University, and wrote
stories, essays, and plays. Her most significant work appeared after she received a grant for research into the
folklore of Floridian Afro-Americans.[4] Between 1934 and
1939 she was married briefly[5] and published five substantial and diversified books which pleased reviewers.[6]
The output slowed abruptly. During the next three years,
she published magazine articles infrequently, but only
one book—a self-consciously written autobiography. Six
more years passed before her next book, in 1948. Suddenly, she was silent. Two years after her final novel was
published, Zora Neale Hurston reappeared in Florida
working as a maid in Riva Alto. Ten years later, she died
penniless in a hospital in Fort Pierce. Her funeral ex-
penses were paid by collection and contribution.

A study of Zora Neale Hurston, writer, properly begins
with Zora Neale Hurston, wanderer. In her autobiog-

raphy, *Dust Tracks on a Road* [7] — in her artful candor and coy reticence, her contradictions and silences, her irrationalities and extravagant boasts which plead for the world to recognize and respect her — one perceives the matrix of her fiction, the seeds that sprouted and the cankers that destroyed.

Contradictions in the autobiography reveal that the content was prepared with concern for its appeal to readers, especially white readers. By reporting her father's frequent warnings that her impudence will cause her to forget to remain in the docile, subservient position to which Southern society assigns Afro-Americans, Miss Hurston created a self-image as a fearless and defiant fighter for her rights. In actuality, however, even white acquaintances were astonished by her apparent indifference to her own dignity or that of other blacks. Expressing surprise at Zora Neale Hurston's refusal to identify with other Afro-Americans struggling for identity, Fannie Hurst rationalized, "Probably this insensibility was due to the fact that her awakening powers and subsequent recognition tended to act as a soporific to her early sufferings." [8] Miss Hurst further ascribed the insouciance to Miss Hurston's optimistic philosophy that "the world will treat you right if you are all right." [9] What Miss Hurst did not perceive, or did not dwell upon, was the obsequious manner of Zora Neale Hurston's apparent indifference to Fannie Hurst's rebukes: "I've been so kicked around all most of my life that your kind of scolding is duck soup to me." [10] The truth is that, in public pronouncements, she ignored ill-treatment from white people.

In *Dust Tracks* she implied that the road of her life was a series of stepping stones generously provided by white patrons. A white man who assisted at her birth became guide and guardian. She never forgot his injunction that she should never "act like a nigger." Because they admired her recitation in elementary school, a group of Northern white visitors sent her books, second-hand clothes, and one hundred pennies. Having recommended her for a maid's job, another white patron then bought her a dress so that she would look more attractive during the interview. Anna Meyer, a trustee of Barnard, helped her become one of the first Negroes to matriculate at the college; Fannie Hurst hired her as secretary; and Franz Boas, a famous anthropologist, secured a scholarship for her. She even boasted that when she called him "Papa," as the other Columbia University students did when he was out of hearing, Boas playfully referred to her as one of his mistakes. In the entire recounting of experiences with white people, she let no shadow of unpleasantness darken her serenity. Once she complained mildly about white customers who propositioned her when she waited on their tables. Hastily, however, she added that she was not offended by the advances but by the paltry sums which were offered. Even when she pointed out that she received less than half of the pay due for her work as a maid for an actress who abandoned her in Baltimore with neither funds nor friends, she rationalized that the experience itself was sufficient reward. She enjoyed the gaiety of the life; and she did not mind the troupe's teasing, for she knew that they were not malicious.[11]

The image of naïve affability has been demolished by Arna Bontemps and Langston Hughes, who have suggested that Zora Neale Hurston deliberately assumed a role designed to gain assistance from white people. Reviewing Zora Neale Hurston's account for her life in *Dust Tracks*, Bontemps observed,

Always in the background stood a line of substantial friends who saw in the exuberant unspoiled colored girl the kind of Negro they wanted to encourage.[12]

More satirically, Hughes wrote,

> In her youth, she was always getting scholarships and things from wealthy white people, some of whom simply paid her just to sit around and represent the Negro race for them, she did it in such a racy fashion. . . . To many of her white friends, no doubt, she was a perfect "darkie," in the nice meaning they give the term—that is, a naïve, childlike, sweet, humorous, and highly colored Negro.[13]

That certainly is the image which remained in the memory of Fannie Hurst, who recalled Miss Hurston's dialect "as deep as the deep south, her voice and laughter the kind I used to hear on the levees of St. Louis." [14] Even when Zora Neale proved hopeless as a secretary because she wrote shorthand which could not be deciphered, typed poorly, and filed illogically, Miss Hurst permitted her to remain as a guest. Summing up, Miss Hurst recalled that Zora Neale lived irresponsibly. She was habitually late; she slept through appointments; she failed to meet her obligations.[15] These failings, Fannie Hurst concluded, constituted part of her charm.[16] They are also, one must add, characteristics identified with the stereotyped "darkie" to whom Hughes alluded.

In contrast to her affable reactions to the white people in her book are her violent rivalries with and antagonisms toward other blacks. Obviously envious of her father's attention to her sister, she unnecessarily reminded readers that the sister did not become famous. She insisted that her brother used her as his wife's slave. She wrote vituperatively about a jealous, "old, fat, black" servant who caused her to be fired and about another "jealous hussy" who tried to kill her. With obvious relish she reported the details of a fight with her stepmother, whom she hated. Dodging a plate thrown at her, Zora Neale grabbed the woman, repeatedly clubbed her in the face, then smashed her head against the wall. When a neighbor investigated, Miss Hurston threw an ax to warn her against interference. Years afterward, she continued, she searched for her stepmother, hoping to resume the battle; but, after finding her, Miss Hurston pitied the aged woman's infirmity. It is psychologically impossible that any human being who would want to kill so many members of her own race should never have resented members of another race. Such a dichotomy of blacks and whites cannot exist except to myopic vision.

Two causes for the myopia suggest themselves. One, the desire to sell her book caused Miss Hurston to conceal her resentment of white Americans. Two, she genuinely enjoyed the paternalism of her white friends.

If the first hypothesis is true, Miss Hurston was a hypocrite; if the second is true, she was immature and insecure.[17] Either hypothesis dissuades one from expecting any perceptive appraisal of the interrelationships of the races in her autobiography, and none is to be found. After ridiculing the chauvinism of Afro-Americans, she turned her attention to the "race problem":

> I have no race prejudice of any kind. My kinfolks, and my "skin-folks" are dearly loved. My own circumference of everyday life is there. But I see their same virtues and vices everywhere I look. So I give you all my right hand of fellowship and love, and hope for the same from you. In my eyesight, you lose nothing by not looking just like me. I will remember you all in my good thoughts, and I ask you kindly to do the same for me. Not only just me. You, who play the zigzag lightning of power over the world, with the grumbling thunder in your wake, think kindly of those who walk in the dust. And you who walk in humble places, think kindly too, of others. There has been no proof in the world so far that you would be less arrogant if

you held the lever of power in your hands. Let us all be kissing-friends. Consider that with tolerance and patience, we godly demons may breed a noble world in a few hundred generations or so. Maybe all of us who do not have the good fortune to meet, or meet again, in this world, will meet at a barbecue.[18]

Obviously, her own magnanimous expression of tolerance for white Americans corrected none of the injustices perpetrated upon black Americans. Furthermore, historically, men have refused to content themselves with blithe hope for a perfect world in "a few hundred generations." As Arna Bontemps wrote with characteristic graciousness, "Miss Hurston deals very simply with the more serious aspects of Negro life in America—she ignores them. She has done right well by herself in the kind of world she found." [19]

But Miss Hurston did not always ignore the serious aspects of the life of Afro-Americans; inexplicably, she denounced some of their efforts to secure equal opportunities in America. In 1950, while black leaders were campaigning vigorously to gain voting rights in the South, she wrote, "I Saw Negro Votes Peddled." [20] She alleged that a Northern Negro organization enticed Negroes to vote as a bloc by promising them Cadillacs, sheets, and towels. She reported that this information came from an unnamed Negro school teacher who worked for the organization and from an unnamed worker who sold his vote.

The truth of her allegations is unimportant. The bartering of votes, a time-established, though socially disapproved practice, is not limited to Afro-Americans, who politically have always exercised a minority voice in America. It is strange, however, that Miss Hurston should have been so opposed to improving voting rights for black people that she would not only imply that they do not deserve those rights but also would base her argument on unsubstantiated allegations from unnamed sources. Moreover, it is incredible that Miss Hurston can have been so gullible as to repeat the charge that Cadillacs were promised as rewards for votes. Even if she actually believed that anyone would naïvely expect to receive a Cadillac or its monetary equivalent for a single vote, she would have damaged her reputation for intelligence less if she had limited her allegations to sheets and towels. So fantastic a charge merely reflects disparagingly upon the one who makes it. Finally, it is absurd that Miss Hurston even pretended to write for an audience which she must have known to be nonexistent. Purportedly, she wrote the article to advise black people to exercise their voting power judiciously, but she published it in the *American Legion Magazine,* a periodical which had few Afro-American readers because it was the official voice of an organization which in 1950 discouraged black membership.

In the same essay Miss Hurston denounced the Fair Employment Practices Committee because she feared that it would enable white people to penetrate Afro-American businesses which "control into the millions in wealth." She opposed those blacks who were suing to have their children admitted to "white" schools: protesting that "free public schools available for Negro children are ably staffed by Negroes," she expressed her fear that continued agitation might cause white teachers to be hired in Negro schools.[21] She scaled the pinnacle of incredibility, however, by blandly asserting that she had derived her knowledge of the "political mechanics of Reconstruction" from a Congressman from Virginia; tutored by this impeccably unbiased source, she charged that, during Reconstruction, all blacks sold their votes for liquor and money.

A year later, in "A Negro Voter Sizes Up Taft,"[22] she

denounced the Democratic Party, which, under Franklin
D. Roosevelt and Harry Truman, had been responsible
for the only significant federal efforts to help Afro-Americans since the early days of Theodore Roosevelt's first
term as President. In 1955 in a letter to the *Orlando
Sentinel,* she protested against the 1954 Supreme Court
declaration that "separate" schools are not equal. The
decision, she wrote, insulted Negroes by implying the
inadequacy of their schools.

It is difficult to hypothesize reasons for such public
pronouncements as these. At times, one wishes to believe
that excessive pride in her race caused her to defend it
against attack without understanding what issues were
involved. For example, it is true that some Afro-American
businesses are valued in millions of dollars. But the threat
which a Fair Employment Practices Commission presented to black business was infinitesimally small in
comparison with the advantages black people might gain
from enforcement of their right to work, be promoted,
and be paid on a salary scale equal to that of their co-
workers. Similarly, it is understandable that a black
person would be insulted by the too common assumption
that black teachers are incompetent and that education
in a black school is inevitably inferior. Personally knowing excellent black teachers, an Afro-American easily
might become furious about such insulting assumptions,
especially since he knows that only remarkably good
teachers could have taught so well under the unfavorable
conditions imposed upon the black schools. Nevertheless,
most black schools were unequal because insufficient
funds prevented their securing the facilities, the equip-
ment, and the numbers of teachers comparable to the
local white institutions.

Or, one rationalizes that her experiences in the all-
black settlement of Eatonville persuaded her to favor the
political, social, and cultural autonomy of a black com-

munity. Or one wonders whether her vision was merely a caste myopia which caused her to admire representatives of any group which she considered socially or economically superior to her. Just as Miss Hurston boasted about her acceptance in the *Social Register* at Barnard, so, in her autobiography, she happily recalled that the pretty Negro socialites in her classes at Morgan Academy permitted her to do their homework. Her gratitude that they even acknowledged her existence by teasing her about her limited wardrobe—only one dress—reminds one of her obsequious reaction to the teasing by the white members of the theatrical troupe.

No single explanation eases the disappointment. The Zora Neale Hurston who takes shape from her autobiography and from the accounts of those who knew her is an imaginative, somewhat shallow, quick-tempered woman, desperate for recognition and reassurance to assuage her feelings of inferiority; a blind follower of that social code which approves arrogance toward one's assumed peers and inferiors but requires total psychological commitment to a subservient posture before one's supposed superiors. It is in reference to this image that one must examine her novels, her folklore, and her view of the Southern scene.

Despite the psychological limitations which color her works, her novels deserve more recognition than they have received. While publishing more books than any Afro-American woman before her—four novels, two collections of folklore, and an autobiography—she was one of the few Southern-born Afro-American writers who have consistently mined literary materials from Southern soil. Gifted with an ear for dialect, an appreciation of the folktale, a lively imagination, and an understanding of feminine psychology, she interwove these materials in deceptively simple stories which exhibit increasing artistic consciousness and her awareness of the shifting tastes in the American literary market.

Her relative anonymity may be blamed on two causes. First, during her most productive period—the 1930s—widespread poverty limited the sale of books. Second, her tales of common people form a seemingly quiet meadow overshadowed by commanding, storm-swept hills on either side. To the rear, in the twenties, stands the exoticism of the Harlem Renaissance—Claude McKay's lurid depictions of Harlem, Wallace Thurman's satirical invective, Langston Hughes's jazz rhythms, and Countee Cullen's melodious chauvinism. On the other side, in the forties, stands the lusty violence of Richard Wright, Frank Yerby, Ann Petry, and Willard Motley. Most of Zora Neale Hurston's stories, in contrast, seem to be quiet quests for self-realization.[23]

Ironic, psychologically perceptive stories first brought her to the attention of Charles S. Johnson and various other editors. "Spunk" and "The Gilded Six-Bits" typify this early work.

"Spunk" reveals the fickleness of the mob. The townspeople praise Spunk Banks when he fearlessly steals Joe Kanty's wife. Then they redirect their praise to Joe when, infuriated by insinuations that he is a coward, he attacks Spunk, who is armed. After Spunk kills Joe, the people play upon his superstitions until he accidentally kills himself. Having murdered two men and destroyed a woman's happiness, the gossips turn to a new subject.

"The Gilded Six-Bits" is equally ironic and poignant. When Joe Banks learns that his wife has been seduced by the gilded six-bit coin of Otis D. Slocum, an arrogant Northern visitor, he begins to treat her as though she is a prostitute. He changes his attitude only after the appearance of their newborn child convinces Joe that he, not Slocum, is actually the father. The story ends ironically. Ignorant of the dissension, a white confectioner who sells Joe a reconciliation gift voices his envy: "Wisht I could be like these darkies. Laughin' all the time. Nothin' worries 'em."

Miss Hurston revealed the same talents in her novels. The simply narrated tales, the credible, likable characters, and the colorful dialogue evoke tenderness and amusement. But in the greater length of the novels, she showed weaknesses. She caricatured less important figures, exaggerated the language, and sacrificed structure for the sake of folktales.

Jonah's Gourd Vine (1934), her first novel, is based on the lives of her parents. Written after she had collected the folktales subsequently published in *Mules and Men* (1935), the novel exemplifies both her strengths and her weaknesses.

The protagonist is John Buddy, upon whom all major actions depend—or more appropriately, upon whom all actions are perpetrated. Passive except when angered, John Buddy does not create situations intentionally. Instead, he reacts to fortune's winds, which most often emanate from the gusty pantings of lustful women.

John Buddy, an illegitimate child born during slavery, lives on the wrong side of the creek. He and his family sharecrop for a white farmer who cheats them. When John Buddy leaves home to escape his abusive stepfather, he goes to his mother's former home at the Pearson plantation on the other side of the creek. While living there, he discovers his dangerous attractiveness to women; but, knowing that he actually loves only Lucy Potts, he marries her despite the objections of her mother, who had hoped for a more prosperous son-in-law. Even Lucy cannot curb his philandering, which consumes the little income he provides. Forced to leave town to escape imprisonment for stealing a hog and attacking Lucy's brother, he wanders South to the recently established all-Negro town of Eatonville, Florida. There, his carpentry and his ministry earn him a position of respect which he continually endangers by his promiscuity. After his wife dies, he marries Hattie, who estranges him from his children. When he is persuaded that she has placed a voodoo curse on him, he divorces her; but, by pleading the injustice of his actions, she wins the sympathy of the townspeople who, refusing either to hire him or to pay what they owe, force him to leave Eatonville. Drifting to Jacksonville, he marries a wealthy woman who helps him reestablish himself as a prosperous preacher. Returning to Eatonville to flaunt his new possessions, however, he is debauched by a young girl. Blinded by shame, he drives in front of a train and is killed.

Because it derives its movement from the action of John Buddy, the plot is logically structured until the second marriage. At that point, desiring to provide poetic justice for her father vicariously, Miss Hurston resorted to melodrama, most apparent in the discovery of the voodoo symbols which motivated John Buddy to divorce his second wife and in the restoration of his fortune.

Although Miss Hurston delineated her protagonists credibly, she exaggerated minor figures. Because she hated her stepmother, Miss Hurston caricatured Hattie, John Buddy's second wife, as a vituperative, ignorant, immoral, vindictive monster. Miss Hurston designed a black girl, Mehaley, as a comic foil for Lucy. Whereas Lucy is intelligent, educated, affectionate, and relatively obedient to her mother's rigid morality, Mehaley is slothful, sensual, and amoral. The contrast reaches a farcical climax in the difference between Lucy's marriage and Mehaley's. Lucy marries John Buddy in a simple, decorous ritual performed with the reverence customary for a sacrament of the church. Mehaley's wedding is delayed first by the tardiness of the bridegroom. It is further delayed by her father, a self-appointed preacher, who refuses to permit an ordained minister to perform the ceremony. After the father prevails and after the bridegroom again imprisons his aching feet in his new shoes, the marriage vows are recited by the illiterate father, who pretends to read the words from a book which he believes to be the Bible but which is actually an almanac. That evening, the bride postpones consummating the marriage until she has satisfied her craving for snuff.

Miss Hurston's predilection for farcical statement frequently distorts the tone of the novel. For instance, while Ned and Amy Crittenden are arguing about the merits of mulattoes, Amy rebukes Ned's argument that Negroes cannot faint:

> "Dass awright. Niggers gwine faint too. May not come in yo' time and it may not come in mine, but way after while, us people is gwine faint jus lak white folks." [24]

The statement ceases to amuse when one realizes that, by attributing it to ex-slaves, Miss Hurston, for the sake of a laugh, denied the existence of slaves who fainted from exhaustion, hunger, and pain.

Exploitation of the exotic weakens the dialogue, which constitutes both the major strength and the major weakness of the novel. Effectively, Miss Hurston created a dialect, or dialects, which, if not authentic, nevertheless suggest a particular level of speech without ridiculing the speaker. The language also exhibits the rural Southern blacks' imaginative, vivid use of metaphor, simile, and invective:

> God was grumbling his thunder and playing the zig-zag lighting thru his fingers.[25]

> "De chickens is cacklin' in de rice and dey say 'Come git it whilst iss fitten' cause t'morrer it may be frost-bitten!' " [26]

> "Seben years ain't too long fuh uh coudar tuh wear uh ruffled bosom shirt." [27]

> "Ah means to beat her 'til she rope lak okra, and den agin Ah'll stomp her 'til she slack lak line." [28]

The verisimilitude of the language is intensified not merely by the dialect and idiom but even by words, such as "lies," "jook," "piney wood rooters," which require definition in the glossary.

But exploiting the appeal of this language, she piled up metaphorical invective to a height difficult for any mortal to attain:

> "And you, you old battle-hammed, slew foot, box-ankled nubbin, you! You ain't nothin' and ain't got nothin' but whut God give uh billy-goat, and then round tryin' tuh hell-hack folks! . . . if you wants tuh fight,—dat's de very corn Ah wants tuh grind. You come grab me now and Ah bet you Ah'll stop *you* from suckin' eggs. . . . Bet Ah'll break uh egg in you! Youse all parts of uh pig! You done got me jus' ez hot ez July jam, and Ah ain't no mo use fuh yuh than Ah is for mah baby shirt. Youse mah race but you sho ain't mah taste. . . .
>
> "Ah'm jus' lak uh old shoe—soft when yuh rain on me and cool me off, and hard when yuh shine on me and git me hot. . . . Ah'm goin tuh Zar, and dat's on de other side of far. . . ." [29]

Each idiom attributed to John Buddy undoubtedly is authentic, but the ratio of metaphors to nonmetaphorical phrases is incredible.

Even less artistically, Miss Hurston sacrificed mood to metaphor in a quarrel between Lucy and John at a tense moment:

> "Ah wouldn't be no man a tall tuh let you' brother uh nobody else snatch uh bed out from under you, mo' special in yo' condition."
>
> "John dat's goin' tuh cause trouble and double, Bud hate you and now you done hit 'im he ain't goin' tuh let his shirt tail touch 'im til he tell it tuh de white folks. . . ."
>
> "Ah ain't goin' tuh no chain-gang. If dey ever git in

behind me, Ah'll tip on cross de good Lawd's green. Ah'll give mah case tuh Miss Bush and let Mother Green stand mah bond."

"Dey liable tuh grab yuh, 'fo' yuh know it."

"Aw les' squat dat rabbit and jump uh 'nother one. You act lack you done cut loose."

"Naw, Ah ain't cut loose but look lak wese tied tuh-gether by uh long cord string and youse at end and Ahm at de other. Way off."

"You kin take in some de slack."

"Don't look lak it."

"Aw, lemme see de caboose uh dat. Less eat dis hog meat and hoe-cake. Jus' 'cause women folks ain't got no big muscled arm and fistes lak jugs, folks claims they's weak vessels, but dass uh lie. Dat piece uh red flannel she got hun 'tween her jaws is equal tuh all de fistes God ever made and man ever seen." [30]

The self-conscious use of metaphor in each utterance weakens the verisimilitude of the otherwise realistic situation.

Miss Hurston's attitude toward interracial relationships in the South seems curiously ambivalent if a reader does not know her social philosophy. On the "poor" side of the creek, John's mother, Amy Crittenden, bitterly denounces slavery, share-cropping, and abusive, unjust white "trash." On the other side of the river, however, John and even Lucy unquestioningly accept Alf Peterson's paternalism. Thus, Miss Hurston imputes all abuses of blacks to lower-class Southern masters, a sentiment which is commercially expedient but false. Except for these opening scenes in Alabama, however, the action of *Jonah's Gourd Vine* is confined to Eatonville, Florida, where the black inhabitants are unaffected by the white people of neighboring communities.

In the novel, Miss Hurston experimented with symbols with varying degrees of success. The image of "Jonah's gourd vine" does not seem to represent John effectively because no Jonah exists. The fact that John Buddy is created by God and is smitten by God furnishes merely a strained analogy. Miss Hurston, however, used a railroad train more effectively. One of the first objects which John sees after he has crossed the creek, the railroad locomotive impresses him as the most powerful, potentially dangerous force he has ever known. More than a machine or even an agent for transportation, however, it symbolizes his sexual awareness. Coming into his consciousness when he first enters a world of heterosexual relationships, it dominates his thoughts and finally destroys him.

Their Eyes Were Watching God (1937) is artistically superior to *Jonah's Gourd Vine*, perhaps because it centers upon a protagonist with whom Miss Hurston could identify fully. In her autobiography, she stated that the novel resulted from her efforts to express a love which she had felt.

Having been forced to marry a much older farmer so that she will not give herself to worthless men, sixteen-year-old Janie runs away with Joe Starks, a charming, ambitious traveling salesman. Although Joe becomes a respected and prosperous leader in Eatonville, Florida, he disappoints her by offering wealth and prestige instead of understanding or love. After his death ends her bigamous relationship of more than twenty years, she finds true love with Teacake, a twenty-five-year-old gambler; but tragically, she is forced to kill Teacake to protect herself when he attacks her in a delerious rage resulting from the rabies he contracted while saving her from a mad dog. Having been acquitted by a jury, she returns to Eatonville to defy the gossips who had predicted that Teacake would abandon her.

Although Miss Hurston wrote *Their Eyes Were*

Watching God in seven months, she demonstrated considerable improvement in her skill as a novelist. Feeling no compulsion to compensate her protagonist for suffering, she developed the story logically. Unfortunately she weakened the story by the highly melodramatic conclusion alleviated only by the romantic sentiment that Teacake still lives in Janie's memory.

Although the death of the protagonist, John Buddy, ends *Jonah's Gourd Vine* and the grief of the protagonist, Janie, concludes *Their Eyes Were Watching God*, neither novel overwhelms a reader with a sense of tragedy. A lighter mood develops, not so much from Miss Hurston's emphasis upon a philosophic acceptance of grief as from her frequent admixtures of comedy and her tendency to report dramatic incidents rather than to involve the reader with the emotions of the characters.

In her second novel Miss Hurston improved her characterization by caricaturing less frequently and by delineating minor characters more carefully. In fact, Nanny, Janie's grandmother, is one of Miss Hurston's most effectively drawn characters. Feeling that life cheated her by enslaving her, Nanny vows that her granddaughter will enjoy the happiness she herself has never known. But seeking to realize herself through her granddaughter, she fails to allow for Janie's personality and aspirations.

Despite her improvements, Miss Hurston did not abandon caricature. Upon the deformed figure of Mrs. Turner, Miss Hurston vented her disgust with middle-class Negroes who distrust or dislike their race. She ridiculed Mrs. Turner's hatred of black-skinned people, Booker T. Washington, Negro doctors and businessmen, and African features. Paradoxically, Miss Hurston was guilty of some of the very prejudices for which she condemned Mrs. Turner. In *Jonah's Gourd Vine* and in *Dust Tracks*, a reader discerns Miss Hurston's obvious admiration of her father's gray eyes and fair skin. Furthermore, she described her protagonist Janie as a fair-skinned woman with "fine hair." In short, despite her impassioned defense of African features as a matter of principle, Miss Hurston's personal biases positioned her nearer to Mrs. Turner than she admitted.

As she improved characterization by restraining her tendency to exaggerate, so she improved dialogue and plot by similar restraint. The dialogue is adorned, not cluttered, with metaphor. The plot is free from pointless farce.

Despite her general improvements, however, Miss Hurston continued to exhibit defects evidencing her inability to complete her transformation from a short-story writer into a novelist. She weakened the plot by a careless shift of point of view and by digressions. Although she narrated most of the story through Janie, she shifted to Nanny in the second chapter in order to abuse the wives of slave owners. (As will be shown later, Miss Hurston's social philosophy did not require submission to Southern wives.)

Miss Hurston committed her most serious structural blunder in chapter six. In the first four chapters she developed the poignant relationship of Janie and Nanny, lyrically explored Janie's personality, and described the brief course of Janie's marriage. In chapter five Miss Hurston altered her tone by abandoning the serious, contemplative dialogue of the earlier chapters in order to imitate the impudent, jovial chatter of the Eatonville folk who spy upon the newcomers, Janie and Joe Starks. In chapter six, however, the longest in the book, Miss Hurston interrupted the narrative in order to include folktales and amusing sketches of local inhabitants. Digressive and unnecessary, the chapter merely suggests that Miss Hurston did not know how to integrate the folk material which she considered essential for local color.

She weakly justified the inclusions as illustrations of the kinds of tales which Janie wishes to hear more often. Later in the story, Miss Hurston introduced similar materials more plausibly as a part of the banter between Teacake and Janie and as the evening or rainy day diversion of the workers with whom Janie and Teacake live.

Either personal insensitivity or an inability to recognize aesthetic inappropriatenesses caused Miss Hurston to besmirch *Their Eyes Were Watching God* with one of the crudest scenes which she ever wrote. While Joe Starks is dying, Janie deliberately provokes a quarrel so that, for the first time, she can tell him how he has destroyed her love. During the early years of their twenty-year relationship, Joe Starks jealously sheltered her excessively; during the later years he often abused her because he resented her remaining young and attractive while he aged rapidly. But in a quarrel or two Janie repaid him in good measure by puncturing his vanity before the fellow townsmen whose respect and envy he wished to command. Never was his conduct so cruel as to deserve the vindictive attack which Janie unleashes while he is dying. For Janie, the behavior seems grotesquely out of character. It is characteristic, however, of Miss Hurston's continual emphasis upon intraracial and intrafamilial hatred. Probably no other Afro-American fiction maker before Richard Wright so fully and frequently described violence within black families.

The thought of *Their Eyes Were Watching God* is more persuasive than that of *Jonah's Gourd Vine*. Through Nanny, Miss Hurston denounced slavery and the wives of slave owners; through Teacake she ridiculed the Southerners' habit of selecting certain blacks as their pets while abusing the others; and through Mrs. Turner she ridiculed Negroes who hate their race. She succeeded best, however, in delineating perceptively a woman whose simple desires mystify the men in her life. Janie merely wishes to live and to love, to laugh and to joke with people. But her husband and her first lover fail to understand that her happiness depends upon love. Because she does not love her first husband, she feels insulted because he wants her to prepare his breakfast, chop wood, and plow in the fields. As long as she loves Joe Starks, however, she is willing to clerk in his store. When she no longer loves him, she resents his wanting her to continue to work. Because she loves Teacake, she works beside him in the fields after he has confessed his loneliness without her. All Janie wants is to love, to be loved, and to share the life of her man. But, like the witch in the Wife of Bath's tale, she first must find a man wise enough to let her be whatever kind of woman she wants to be.

Miss Hurston's most accomplished achievement in fiction is *Moses, Man of the Mountain* (1939), which provided a format in which she could best utilize her talents for writing satire, irony, and dialect. Because Miss Hurston introduced the novel by discussing the popularity of the Moses legend among people of African descent, some critics have adjudged the novel merely the transcription of a folktale. That erroneous assumption may explain, for instance, Robert Bone's failure to discuss the book among Miss Hurston's other novels.

Miss Hurston must be credited, however, with artistic inventiveness. Her style so closely resembles John Erskine's satiric modernizations of the stories of Tristan and Helen of Troy and Galahad that one immediately suspects Miss Hurston's intention to re-create Moses in similar manner.

If she had written nothing else, Miss Hurston would deserve recognition for this book. For once, her material and her talent fused perfectly. Her narrative deficiencies are insignificant, for the reader knows the story. Her ridicule, caricature, and farce are appropriate. The monstrous Hattie of *Jonah's Gourd Vine* and Mrs. Turner of *Their Eyes Were Watching God* reappear aptly in the jealous, accursed Miriam, who actually becomes a sympathetic figure after she has been cursed with leprosy. Finally, attuned to folk psychology, Miss Hurston gave the Hebrew slaves an authenticity that they lack in the solemn Biblical story.

Of course, Afro-Americans previously had recognized and used in song and story the analogy between the enslaved Hebrews and the enslaved blacks. Before a black writer could treat the materials satirically in the manner of Miss Hurston, however, Afro-Americans needed to achieve sufficient detachment to be able to laugh at members of their race. Dunbar had been misunderstood when he had laughed three decades earlier. Although Countee Cullen, Langston Hughes, and Wallace Thurman had mimicked the blacks of Harlem, they had been censured by sensitive Afro-Americans who feared that the ridicule would hamper their efforts to be accepted in the dominant culture. By writing about Moses, however, Miss Hurston set her story so far in the past that she could not be criticized for lampooning contemporary Afro-Americans even though they obviously served as prototypes for her Hebrew slaves.

In Miss Hurston's story, Moses is the illegitimate son of Pharoah's daughter. Therefore, like the mulattoes who governed the National Association for the Advancement of Colored People during Miss Hurston's adult years, he is suspected of being different and, possibly, treacherous. He is even criticized for having married a fair-skinned foreigner of royal blood, who is suspected of judging herself socially superior to the ex-slaves.

Since, according to Miss Hurston, Moses is not related to Miriam, who fabricated the tale about the princess to conceal the embarrassing truth that she fell asleep while watching the basket in which her brother lay concealed, neither Miriam nor Aaron can justly claim authority during the exodus. But, obsessed with a desire for prestige, they continually attempt to subvert Moses' power. Like some antagonists of Afro-Americans, the Egyptian pharoah, by deceit and by force, strives to preserve the old order—the slave labor—which his nobles demand. The Hebrew slaves are the same people whom Miss Hurston, gaily but sympathetically, had lampooned previously in her anecdotes about "my people, my people." They are the Eatonville gossips "way down in Egypt land." Bickering continually about food, water, habitat, and every irritation, they nostalgically recall the days in Egypt: "There we was sitting down every day to a big pot of meat and bread . . . we don't care if they did work us some. We would much rather die tired than to die hungry." [31]

The chief art of the book is the abundant comedy. Humor emerges even from the mere contrast of the bombastic speech of the Egyptians, the realistic speech of the educated people, and the credible dialect of the slaves. But a good joke, at best, is merely a joke. Miss Hurston's joke entertains readers but does not comment significantly on life or people.

In her final novel, *Seraph on the Suwanee* (1948), Miss Hurston for the first time focused upon white protagonists, in a work so stylistically different from her earlier efforts that it reveals her conscious adjustment to the tastes of a new generation of readers. Although *Seraph* is Hurston's most ambitious novel and her most artistically competent, its prolonged somberness causes many readers to yearn for the alleviating farce and carefree gaiety of the earlier works.

Even as a child, Arvay Henson, of an impoverished Florida family, suffers neurotic insecurity because her older sister has won every battle of their bitter sibling rivalry. When her sister marries Carl Middleton, whom

Arvay loves, Arvay withdraws from life. Vowing to become a missionary as soon as she has attained the required age, she refuses to entertain male visitors; if they persist, she frightens them away by pretending to have a fit. Despite her reputation, Jim Meserve, the handsome scion of a bankrupt Virginia family, courts her and, by raping her, conquers her.

From the beginning, Arvay's insecurity threatens their marriage. She fears that Jim will love her sister, even though the sister is married. When their son proves unquestionably to be an idiot, she fears that Jim will blame the child's abnormality on traits inherited from her family. When Jim exhibits his pride in their first daughter, she jealously resents the love he gives to the child. Even the birth of a third child, a son, brings no comfort.

Imagining that everyone and everything threaten her security, she seeks to erect a wall around her husband and her children. When troubles occur, generally because she will not look at life rationally, she blames other people; actually she fears that they may breach the wall and take Jim or one of the children from her. First, she attacks Joe, a black man whom Jim uses as a helper and a pet. By curtness and overt hostility, she compels Joe and his family to move from the shack behind Jim's house. When the Portuguese Corregios move into the shack, Arvay, who dislikes foreigners as much as she dislikes black people, directs her antagonistic fears toward them. When Earl, her older son, proves so dangerously insane that Jim proposes committing him to an asylum or at least sending him away, Arvay imputes Earl's eccentricities to the Corregios's presence. Arvay dislikes Jim's fondness for Mr. Corregio; and, when Mrs. Corregio, an excellent cook, sends Arvay recipes for Jim's favorite dishes, Arvay suspects Mrs. Corregio of trying to entice Jim. She fears that Jim is romantically interested in the older Corregio girl, and she even resents her children's friendship with Felicia, the younger daughter.

Although she has lacked material possessions, she has maintained her sense of superiority to Negroes and farmers by idealizing her family. When she revisits them, however, she is astonished to perceive their shabbiness, uncleanliness, and slovenliness. Realizing that Jim has rescued her from that kind of life, she understands that she must continue to have his protection; but because of her neurotic anxiety, she inexorably drives him from her. When Earl, her demented child, attacks the older Corregio girl, Arvay begs Jim to save the boy; but, after a posse has killed Earl to save Jim's life, Arvay accuses Jim of failing to protect his son. Similarly, because Arvay wishes to preserve her youth by ignoring her children's growth, she accuses Jim of seeking to steal their love when he helps the son enter college and helps the daughter defy her mother's objections to her marriage.

After the children have left home, Arvay quarrels with Jim incessantly because her psychotic fear of losing him conjures daily evidences that Jim desires to desert her. Finally, he does leave.

Although Jim has assured her that he will return as soon as she understands his love, Arvay sinks into an almost catatonic state, from which she is roused only by the necessity of visiting her dying mother. Shocked into reality by a second exposure to the squalor of her family's habitat, Arvay begins to understand that Jim removed her from those conditions because he loved her. Finally comprehending that his love has caused him to work for her and to face dangers recklessly in order to win her admiration, she returns to him confident that she has found her desire, "an eternal refuge and everlasting welcome of heart to rest and rely on." [32]

When Robert Bone complains that the novel is less interesting than *Jonah's Gourd Vine* or *Their Eyes Were Watching God*, one must assume that he is lamenting the loss of the exotic metaphors and folktales. Although *Seraph* is not a black story in white face, it significantly parallels the earlier novels in most respects. For instance, despite differences of dialect and ambition, the protagonists of *Seraph* have their prototypes in *Their Eyes Were Watching God*. Like Janie, Arvay Henson, a woman of the lower caste of Southern society, is searching for love. Like Teacake, Jim courts charmingly and boldly; like Joe Starks, he dedicates himself to providing comfort for his mate. Even the familiar vituperative caricatures recur—in Arvay's slovenly sister Larraine and her husband, Carl Middleton.

If the differences in race are ignored, *Seraph* is distinguished from the earlier novels chiefly by Miss Hurston's emphasis upon the protagonist's psychological dilemma, more specific and more realistic descriptions of locale, more lurid details in the accounts of sexual relationships, and the omission of farcical incidents and of folktales. Each of the first three heightens the dramatic or at least the melodramatic quality of the story; therefore, the absence of the exotic charm of the humor, the language, and the folklore seems the only possible basis for a complaint that this novel is less interesting than earlier ones.

To defend *Seraph* against the unwarranted objection, however, is not to imply that the novel is Miss Hurston's most successful. Even though Miss Hurston structured the novel more competently than any other, she betrayed her intention by her thought, and she betrayed her ability by her tone. A writer who proposes a psychological study must do more than describe a behavior pattern and report or dramatize neurosis; he must interpret the relationship of the two in such a way that a reader recognizes that the action is a manifestation or a result of the emotional state. In other words, the author must comprehend psychological complexity sufficiently that he not only supplies an objective correlative but also demonstrates that it actually is a correlative. Because

Miss Hurston was herself impulsive rather than rational and because she approached people intuitively rather than analytically, she failed to control her materials.

One incident in particular evidences Miss Hurston's weakness. Jim playfully seizes a poisonous snake which he holds in such a way that he cannot be bitten. But as Arvay watches in horror, Jim loses control. Although she knows that he needs her help, Arvay cannot move. After a black man has helped Jim destroy the snake, Jim reproves Arvay for failing to understand his love.

All actions and all thoughts in the incident are probable, but Miss Hurston failed to appraise their interrelationships. What Jim wants Arvay to realize is that, like a small boy, he grabbed the snake to impress her with his daring and, thereby, to elicit her admiration. In addition, Miss Hurston wished to suggest that, by failing to act, Arvay demonstrated to Jim that he cannot depend upon her when he needs help. Nevertheless, most readers will excuse Arvay for not perceiving that Jim's seizing a snake indicates his emotional need for her. As has been stated, Miss Hurston here and elsewhere failed to correlate the actions with the emotional states of consciousness.

Furthermore, she betrayed her talent by adopting a new tone. To write a best seller for the forties, she added sex and sensation to her usual fare. In her earlier works, by restrained emotion and detachment, she had made the griefs pathetic but bearable; in *Seraph*, however, she plunged readers into the deep and bitter emotions of a sick world. Doubtlessly, she proved to be a competent guide to that world. But since many other writers can guide such tours, it is regrettable that Miss Hurston did not restrict her tours to the world of the healthy.

Although an examination of her novels is the chief focus of this study, no consideration of Zora Neale Hurston would be complete without an appraisal of her work as folklorist. *Mules and Men* (1935) and *Tell My Horse* (1938), as well as her autobiography, clearly evidence Zora Neale Hurston's talents as a reporter and her weaknesses as a scholar. Both books resulted from research grants which were awarded to enable Miss Hurston to gather folklore of Africans in the United States and the Caribbean. Although William Wells Brown had published folktales in *My Southern Home* (1880) and a few Afro-American writers had used folklore, no Afro-American before Zora Neale Hurston had compiled and published a significant, substantial collection of folklore.

The more valuable of her two collections, *Mules and Men*, includes folklore of Afro-Americans in Florida and in Louisiana. The first section of the work consists of folktales gathered from Florida. Many of the stories have only slight import. These range from tall tales (about unusually hot temperatures or about animals' extraordinary feats of strength or speed) to more familiar classics about tests required to defeat the devil or to win a girl. Other tales, however, furnish deeper social significance. Some ridicule Afro-Americans' ignorance and laziness or praise their cunning. Others indirectly criticize injustice in America by suggesting mythic reasons for the burdens placed on black people.

The usual hero is John, whom Miss Hurston carefully distinguished from John Henry, a creation—so Miss Hurston reported—of white storytellers. The black folk hero John is superhumanly strong and fast, and he is extremely cunning. Although somewhat awed by God, he glories in his ability to outwit a white man or the devil. The rabbit, the animal self-image of the Afro-American in much of his folklore, appears in surprisingly few tales. Miss Hurston has explained that native Floridians tell their stories about the gopher, the Florida equivalent of the rabbit.

The second section of *Mules and Men* recounts Miss Hurston's experiences while learning voodoo, or hoodoo, the religious rites and magic which the slaves brought from Africa to the Western Hemisphere. Miss Hurston described the hoodoo men, the initiation rites, and the "charms" in fascinating detail.

Although *Mules and Men* is interesting, it is disappointingly superficial for the reader who desires more than entertainment. Miss Hurston repeatedly identified herself as an anthropologist, but there is no evidence of the scholarly procedures which would be expected from a formally trained anthropologist or researcher in folklore. Instead of classifying or analyzing tales, she merely reported them in the chronological order and the manner in which they had been told to her. Furthermore, she failed to ask or to answer essential questions. For instance, her internship as a witch doctor required her to prescribe charms and cures. Although a reader eagerly wishes to learn some results of her treatments, Miss Hurston dropped the matter after reciting the details of the prescriptions.

It cannot be said in her defense that Miss Hurston regarded the folklore with the eye of a novelist rather than a scholar. Although interested in the personalities of the storytellers, the idiom spoken by Afro-Americans, and the banter and the flirtation which accompany and encompass the storytelling sessions, she did not attempt to transform the folktale into art, as Joel Chandler Harris did with the Uncle Remus materials or as Charles Waddell Chesnutt did in "The Goophered Grapevine." Perhaps Miss Hurston neglected these matters because she was overly concerned with her major topic—Zora Neale Hurston, who travels, who learns to collect material, who is initiated into strange rituals, and who enjoys her visits. Nevertheless, despite the superficiality which limits its scholarly importance, *Mules and Men* is an enjoyable work of competent journalism, which offers valuable insight into a class of people and a way of life.

Tell My Horse (1938) reflects even more disastrously

Miss Hurston's regrettable inability to distinguish the important from the unimportant, the significant from the trivial. Although she had proposed a study of the voodoo of Haiti and the West Indies, she produced instead a travelogue of her experience, her reactions to the people, and her descriptions of the country. Such travelogues attain significance only if they have been prepared by political scientists or sociologists capable of evaluating their experiences. Miss Hurston not only lacked such training, but she also proved herself to be irritatingly naïve.

For more than a decade, the American government's policy and practice in Haiti had provoked controversy. In 1915 American military forces had occupied Haiti and coerced the government to sign a constitution which gave America control of the economy and the police force. The American government justified its action by alleging that it had been forced to intervene in Haitian affairs in order to protect the Americans living there. Many Afro-American intellectuals, however, charged that the American government merely invented this pretext to disguise its mercenary intention to exploit a nation of free colored people. One of the most vociferous opponents of American intervention was James Weldon Johnson, secretary of the National Association for the Advancement of Colored People. Having served several years as a consul for the American government, Johnson had acquired firsthand knowledge of revolutions in Central American countries. Denying that the Haitian government had requested the intervention,[33] Johnson accused the American government of imperialism and American soldiers of unwarranted cruelty.[34] During the occupation the Marines killed more than three thousand Haitians, many of them unarmed. Johnson's charges had sufficient validity that Warren Harding used them as an issue in the Presidential campaign in 1920.[35]

Because American military forces still occupied the island during the 1920s, Haitians and Afro-Americans continued to protest. But, in the 1930s, Zora Neale Hurston, an American traveler who knew little about politics and who previously had demonstrated no noteworthy perceptivity, condemned the Haitian people for ignorance and destructive self-deception,[36] and asserted that, for their own good, they needed to be disciplined and ruled by a beneficent American government. Intelligent Haitians, she said, rejoiced when American Marines landed because they brought peace.[37] She described the Haitians as innately cruel and sadistic people, an allegation which must have surprised Johnson, who found them kind and polite.[38] To support her charge of cruelty, she said that she saw some peasants mercilessly prod donkeys with sticks, and she knew that peasants also bound the legs of live chickens and carried them for miles until the chickens lost consciousness.[39] She ridiculed a Haitian native's countercharge that Americans might be considered cruel because they boil live lobsters. While she castigated an entire black nation because some people mistreated chickens and donkeys, she ignored the actions of her fellow countrymen, whose moral superiority she praised. In lynchings, Americans burned and tortured to death three thousand black human beings within a period of thirty years. As usual, Miss Hurston vilified those whom her public would permit her to consider her social inferiors. As might be expected, she extolled the white Americans she met in Haiti.

Tell My Horse has value only in Miss Hurston's account of Jamaican and Haitian folktales and voodoo customs, which are more fascinating than those of *Mules and Men* because they are less familiar to American readers. Especially intriguing are the descriptions of the witch doctors and of Zombies (the living dead). Miss Hurston even included a photograph purported to be that of a Zombie. *Tell My Horse* reveals Miss Hurston's usual talent for gathering material, her skill in reporting it, and her characteristic inability to interpret it.

Because of her simple style, humor, and folklore, Zora Neale Hurston deserves more recognition than she ever earned. But, superficial and shallow in her artistic and social judgments, she became neither an impeccable raconteur nor a scholar. Always, she remained a wandering minstrel. It was eccentric but perhaps appropriate for her to return to Florida to take a job as a cook and maid for a white family [40] and to die in poverty. She had not ended her days as she once had hoped—a farmer among the growing things she loved. Instead she had returned to the level of life which she proposed for her people.

Notes

1 – Jean Toomer

1. Letter from Waldo Frank to Jean Toomer, April 25, 1922. This and all letters and unpublished manuscripts referred to in this study are located in the Jean Toomer Collection at Fisk University, Nashville, Tennessee.

2. Quoted by Toomer in letter to Frank, July 25, 1922.

3. Letter from Frank to Toomer, July 26, 1922.

4. Letter from Lola Ridge to Toomer, November 19, 1922.

5. Letter from Sherwood Anderson to Toomer, December 22, 1922.

6. Letter from Anderson to Toomer, undated, ca. 1922–23.

7. Letter from Allen Tate to Toomer, November 7, 1923.

8. William Stanley Braithwaite, "The Negro in American Literature," in *The New Negro: An Interpretation*, ed. A. Locke (New York, 1925), p. 44.

9. Letter from John McClure to Anderson, January 29, 1924.

10. Letter from Anderson to Toomer, January 3, 1924.

11. Mrs. Marjorie C. Toomer ascribes the limited sales to the fact that Boni and Liveright printed an insufficient number of books to meet the demand. She recalls that when *Cane* appeared, she was working at The Sunwise Turn, a selective bookshop in New York City. The requests for the book exhausted all efforts to keep it in stock, and the demand continued even after copies were no longer available from the publication.

12. In a diary, Toomer wrote in 1930, "Something in me has always been convinced that I am a child of great destiny,

that I have a star, that I am being led on by it towards a great fulfillment."

13. From about 1927 until at least 1946 or 1947, Jean Toomer outlined, sketched, or detailed his life in several autobiographies. At least twice—in 1929 and during the 1940s—Toomer hoped to have an autobiography accepted by a publisher. The problem of distinguishing one draft of the autobiography from another is complicated by various facts: Toomer left some drafts incomplete, failed to date some of the writing, and used identical titles for different versions. This much seem certain. He completed at least one autobiography prior to 1929. Although the tentative title was "Incredible Journey," it was probably retitled "Earth Being" before it was submitted for publication. This autobiography was drafted while Toomer lived in New York and Chicago. About 1930 Toomer revised "Earth Being." An abortive revision may be the manuscript of a partial draft which is undated but which was probably composed about 1930. At some time after 1931, and probably during the early 1930s, he privately printed a brief autobiography, A Fiction and Some Facts, in which he focused on his racial identity and his attitudes about race. In 1936 he wrote an autobiography to explain his relationship to George Gurdjieff. During the late 1930s and early 1940s, he completed an autobiography while living in Chicago and at Mill House in Pennsylvania. This autobiography was probably entitled "Incredible Journey." During the same period he drafted an "Outline of an Autobiography," which may have been the outline for "Incredible Journey" or for a final version. He submitted one version for publication in 1929; his final version was rejected in 1946.

There are some significant differences between the various versions. For instance, in one, Toomer writes affectionately of his father and suggests that his father's mother may have been a slave. In another, he scarcely mentions his father but devotes considerable detail to a discussion of his grandparents.

Only fragments of one version exist in a published form which is readily accessible: "Chapters from Earth Being,"

The Black Scholar, 2 (January 1971), 3–14. For the reader who may have the interest and opportunity to examine the unpublished versions in the library of Fisk University, I shall use the following code: "Autobiographical Draft," the partial draft prepared about 1930; "Earth Being," the version composed while he lived in New York and Chicago, probably the earliest complete manuscript; "Autobiography (1936)," the version in which he emphasizes his intellectual development and his relationship to Gurdjieff; "Incredible Journey," the version prepared while he lived in New York and Pennsylvania, possibly the final complete version among the Toomer papers at Fisk; "Outline of an Autobiography," the draft and outline which probably constituted the skeleton of his final version.

14. In "Outline of an Autobiography" Toomer wrote, "It was characteristic of me to appear callous as to a thing which meant unbearably much to me. Thus I seemed almost hard-boiled about my mother's heartbreak and death."

15. Somewhat unconvincingly, Toomer attempted to rationalize his departure from Wisconsin by explaining that his love for a young woman made it impossible to endure separation from her. Although he had known her since the family's return to Washington in 1909, he had fallen in love with her that preceding Christmas when he had gone to her house to visit her sister, whom he had courted ardently during his junior year in high school and whom he had visited regularly during the preceding summer. When the end of the Christmas holidays forced their return to school, Toomer wrote in "Outline of an Autobiography," his thoughts accompanied her to Boston and remained there although his body continued to attend classes in Madison, Wisconsin. After leaving Madison, however, he seems to have made no effort to visit Boston.

16. The facts about Toomer come from his unpublished autobiographies and letters. Cautious interpretation is, therefore, necessary. Normally, however, such interpretation is not difficult, for rationalizations and apologies are made apparent by factual discrepancies. For instance, this dramatic account of his withdrawal from college appears in "Autobiography

(1936)." In "Outline," he states more simply, and more credibly, that, already bored by school, he withdrew when excitement about the war diverted his attention even further.

17. In "Autobiography (1936)."

18. Toomer subsequently explained his views about religion. In "Autobiography (1936)," he postulated that religion is a "way of experiencing characterized by devotion. Philosophy is devotion to truth. Religion is devotion to Being. Art is devotion to life."

19. Letter from Frank to Toomer, April 3, 1922.

20. Two decades later Richard Wright developed a similar theme in *Native Son*. The differences are significant. Reared in an upper-middle-class society and somewhat contemptuous of the laboring classes, Toomer explained the antisocial behavior as an intelligent youth's conscious repudiation of the mores of the dominant culture. A product of the laboring classes, Wright regarded Bigger Thomas's antisocial behavior as a subliminal reaction to conditioning by the society which rejected him.

21. Letter from Toomer to Frank, July 19, 1922.

22. Robert Bone, *The Negro Novel in America*, rev. ed. (New Haven, Conn., 1965), p. 88.

23. The current debate about *Cane*'s status as a novel seems pointless except as it reveals the willingness of literary historians to cling to their beliefs without regard for facts. Certainly *Cane* can be said to have organization. It also resembles Sherwood Anderson's *Winesburg, Ohio*, which Toomer had read before he went to Sparta, Georgia. Nevertheless, the fact is that Toomer composed the various pieces separately and sent them individually to editors of magazines. By the summer of 1922, as he explained in a letter to Waldo Frank dated July 19, he "had the impulse to collect [his] sketches and poems under the title perhaps of Cane." Anderson, who saw individual pieces as Toomer sent them to the *Double Dealer* and who offered to help secure publication, never referred to the proposed work as a novel. Anderson would have been too knowledgeable to do so; for, in December 1922, when Toomer first informed him of the proposed book, Toomer stated that he was "writing three new pieces,

and putting *Cane* (my book) together." (No. 43 in Jean Toomer Collection at Fisk University.) In the introduction to *Cane*, Waldo Frank referred to *Cane* only as "a book" even though he emphasized the fact that a reader sees a complex form evolve from the apparent chaos. Most persuasive of all, in addition to the letters in which Toomer describes his organizational preferences to Frank and to his publisher, is the fact that when Toomer proposed a second volume based on black and brown life in Washington, Horace Liveright expressed his regret that Toomer was not yet proposing a novel. (Letter from Liveright to Toomer, March 12, 1923.) It is ironic that while historians bemuse themselves with explanations of their theories that *Cane* is a novel, Toomer suffered during the late twenties and early thirties because publishers insisted on his sending them a novel rather than another book like *Cane*.

24. Toomer, "Karintha," *Cane* (New York, 1923), p. 1.

25. Ibid., pp. 1–2.

26. Ibid., p. 4.

27. Ibid., p. 5.

28. Ibid., p. 4.

29. Letter from Elizabeth Loguen to Toomer, February 14, 1924.

30. Toomer, "Becky," *Cane*, p. 8.

31. Ibid.

32. Ibid., p. 10.

33. Ibid., p. 12.

34. Toomer, "Fern," *Cane*, pp. 24–25.

35. Ibid., p. 32.

36. Ibid., p. 33.

37. Ibid., p. 32. As the work of Toomer is being studied more widely, numerous explications are developing for various stories. In one of the more recent, Hargis Westerfield, emphasizing the Judeo-Christian atmosphere of "Fern," has suggested the possibility of an analogy with the Immaculate Conception in the mystic experience described by Toomer. See *CLA Journal* 14 (March 1971), 274–76.

38. Toomer, "Carma," *Cane*, p. 18.

39. Ibid., pp. 19–20.

40. Toomer, "Esther," *Cane*, pp. 38–39.

41. Ibid., p. 48.

42. Knowledge of the friendship between Toomer and Frank has caused some critics to find influences of Frank's *Holiday* in *Cane*. Although both books appeared in 1923, and direct correspondence between the two would seem to indicate mutual indebtedness, Toomer had begun writing the stories and sketches of *Cane* during the winter of 1921–22. By mid-July of 1922, even though he had not yet seen a sketch in print, he had completed most of the sketches. "Box Seat" and "Bona and Paul" were apparently written later.

In July, Frank, who had seen much of Toomer's work, wrote Toomer that he was planning a book about Negroes. During the remainder of the summer, Frank probably developed that idea. In mid-September or, more probably, in October, Toomer and Frank visited South Carolina so that Frank could evaluate the authenticity of the atmosphere for his book. January 16, 1923, Frank wrote Toomer to ask him to review *Holiday*. Eight days earlier Boni and Liveright had accepted *Cane*.

This is not intended to imply that Frank did not influence Toomer's style. Sherwood Anderson, who was reading Toomer's manuscripts avidly during the fall of 1922, suspected that he detected such influence inToomer's changing style. It should not be assumed carelessly, however, that Toomer merely imitated *Holiday*. In fact, it is as valid to suggest that Toomer was influenced by the style of Sherwood Anderson. In a letter written to Anderson in December 1922, Toomer emphasized the degree to which Anderson's *Winesburg, Ohio* and *The Triumph of the Egg* had impressed him. Moreover, while explaining Toomer's lyricism, John McClure, in a letter to Anderson, added his belief that Anderson's talent was the same kind of lyricism.

43. Toomer, "Theatre," *Cane*, pp. 92–93.

44. In a revised version intended for stage presentation Toomer further developed the religious symbolism. The curtain closes on the tableau of Carrie K holding Father John, who is dying. The inspirational image of Madonna with

Child is distorted into the black reality of a childless virgin comforting a senile savior dying of old age.

45. "Song of the Son," *Cane*, p. 21.

46. "Storm Ending," *Cane*, p. 90.

47. "Georgia Portrait," *Cane*, p. 50.

48. Letter from McClure to Anderson, January 29, 1924. No. 53 in the Jean Toomer Collection at Fisk University.

49. Letter from Toomer to Anderson, December, 1922. Walter Pinchback suggests that, in Georgia, Toomer lived near relatives of the Toomers. The authenticity of the report, however, is questionable. There is no reference to such a reunion in any of Toomer's correspondence during the period. The more persuasive possibility is that Walter Pinchback's hazy memory inferred erroneous conclusions from the mere fact that Toomer worked in Georgia, the state from which Nathan Toomer had come and to which he reportedly had returned.

50. Letter from Toomer to McClure, June 30, 1922.

51. Letter from Toomer to Frank, July 25, 1922.

52. Letter from Toomer to *The Liberator*, August 19, 1922.

53. Letter from Toomer to Anderson, December 1922.

54. Letter from Toomer to Horace Liveright, March 9, 1923.

55. Letter from Toomer to Liveright, 1923.

56. Letter from Toomer to Godo Remszhardt, August 23, 1930.

57. Letter from Toomer to *The New Freeman*, September 1930.

58. Letter from Toomer to Nancy Cunard, February 8, 1932.

59. Toomer did not mention that he had failed to correct several others who held the same "misconception" about his race. These are only a few: Sherwood Anderson, whose praise has been mentioned; John McClure, who identified him to Anderson as a Negro; Alain Locke, who praised his early writing; Claude McKay, who was interested in learning more about the young Negro submitting excellent work to *The Liberator*; Mae Wright, who met him in Harper's Ferry and who received his inspirational messages about the need

to be proud of Negro racial ancestry; W. E. B. DuBois, who harshly reviewed *Cane*, which he believed to be a work by a Negro; Elizabeth Loguen, who consoled him by assuring him that DuBois was merely jealous. Frank, however, became the culprit.

60. The most succinct statement is found in A *Fiction and Some Facts*, published privately, probably after 1930. Toomer wrote, "I am not prepared to state as fact that there was, or that there was not, some Negro or Indian blood in the family. . . . However, no other member of his [P. B. S. Pinchback's] immediate family was, or was regarded as, a Negro." (p. 4.) Carelessly one might suppose this to be merely an incredible allegation by which Toomer hoped to deceive the friends and acquaintances who read his booklet. Attention needs to be given, however, to the possibility that Toomer actually was uncertain. Several facts support this possibility. First, it is true that some Afro-Americans, who have no wish to deny their ancestry, cannot verify the racial identities of certain grandparents, even when the actual identity of the grandparents is known. Since some Afro-Americans cannot be distinguished physically from white Americans, a white American could pass for an Afro-American. Although too many Americans contemptuously presume that no one would identify himself as Afro-American unless required to, the ability to pass undoubtedly benefited some whites who chose to marry and live with identifiable nonwhites in states where laws prohibited interracial marriages. In such situations, no one would think to question the racial identification until some descendant—a generation or two removed—raised this issue. By that time trustworthy records probably would not exist; there would be only the faulty memories about a matter which had not been carefully examined.

In further defense of Toomer, one must add that in 1930, in a diary not intended for publication, he privately repeated his uncertainty. After explaining that neither his conditioning nor his temperament would classify him as either white or colored, he concluded that he could neither deny that he had Negro blood nor prove that he had it: "I do not *know*

I possess it; . . . it is a carrying on of my grandfather's statement that he had negro blood. . . ."

Even more persuasive is the corroboration by Walter Pinchback, Toomer's uncle, who, in an interview published in *The Baltimore Afro-American* newspaper on December 1, 1934, stated that there was no way of determining whether P. B. S. Pinchback was white or colored. Walter Pinchback, however, further confused the issue by adding that Toomer's father "was also fair, although known as colored."

61. In "The Crock of Problems," however, Toomer denies that he attempted to pass for white. He states that a "passing" Negro avoids contact with other Negroes, constantly fears identification, and begins to hate Negroes. Toomer denies that he was guilty of any of these. Sometimes, he writes, he identified himself as Negro, and sometimes he did not.

62. Frank to Toomer, undated letter, 1923 or early in 1924.

63. Letter from Toomer to John McClure, June 30, 1922.

64. In "Earth Being."

65. In "Autobiography (1936)."

66. Letter from Gorham Munson to Toomer, March 4, 1932.

67. Letter from Kenneth Macgowan to Toomer, Sept. 22, 1923.

68. Langston Hughes, *The Big Sea* (New York, 1940), p. 241.

69. Ibid., p. 242.

70. Letter from Toomer to McClure, July 22, 1922.

71. Letter, July 29, 1922. No. 3346 in Toomer Collection.

72. Letter from McClure to Toomer, May 9, 1924.

73. In *The Little Review*, 11 (1926), pp. 3–7.

74. Interestingly, in those dramas developed recently according to a black aesthetic, contemporary black dramatists depend heavily upon pantomimes of the activities of the lives of Afro-Americans.

75. Letter from Fred Leighton to Toomer, August 15, 1928.

76. Letter from Munson to Toomer, March 19, 1928.

77. Letter from Paul Rosenfeld to Toomer, March 29, 1928.

78. In 1928, he was rumored to be married to an "E. A." When this proved false, another woman—with whom he had a romance in 1927—tried ardently but unsuccessfully to lead him to the altar.

79. Letter from Toomer to Katherine Flinn, September 20, 1927.

80. Letter from Toomer to B. G. Tobey of Brentano's, April 7, 1929.

81. Letter from Ogden Nash to Toomer, January 24, 1930.

82. Some of the aphorisms are provocative:

> One must glow before he can glorify.
> We live; therefore we are in trouble.
> He who shuts out life is by life shut out.
> We learn the rope of life by untying its knots.
> We who talk of knowledge of the universe
>   cannot sense the nature of an apple.
> It is sometimes necessary to teach the
>   brain by application to the bottom.
> To know a day's name is not to know
>   the life thereof.
> His knowledge may be your superstition.
> Science is a system of exact mysteries.
> A child is a cosmos approaching adult chaos.
> People mistake their limitations for high standards.

Many, however, are tedious or abstruse.

83. Letter from Toomer to Harrison Smith, September 27, 1932.

84. Letter from Toomer to Smith, September 1933.

85. Ibid.

86. Toomer is inconsistent about the time or times of the experience. He implied that the first vision occurred while he was walking beside a lake near the campus of the University of Wisconsin in 1914. Later he placed an experience in New York while he was attending New York University in 1917. The most influential vision, however, seems to have

occurred at an elevated railway station sometime between 1917 and 1924.

87. Letter from Toomer to a chaplain at Vassar College, November 13, 1948.

88. Letter from Toomer to Howard Schubert, December 14, 1949.

89. Ibid.

90. Letter from Toomer to "Sandy," undated, 1951. "Sandy" was Floyd M. Sandberg, the son-in-law of Marjorie Content Toomer.

2 – Countee Cullen

1. Stephen Bronz, *Roots of Negro Racial Consciousness: Three Harlem Poets* (New York, 1964), p. 47.

2. Countee Cullen, "After a Visit," *The Medea and Some Poems* (New York, 1935).

3. Cullen, "The Wish," *The Black Christ and Other Poems* (New York, 1929).

4. Collected in *Color* (New York, 1925).

5. Beulah Rheimherr, "Countee Cullen: A Biographical and Critical Study" (M.A. thesis, University of Maryland, 1960).

6. In July 1934 a public announcement was made that Cullen had been appointed head of the English Department of Dillard University in New Orleans, Louisiana. See *Opportunity*, 12 (July 1934), 221.

7. "Surrounded by His Books Countee Cullen is Happy," interview with Countee Cullen, *Christian Science Monitor*, October 23, 1925, p. 6.

8. Garetta Busey, "Books," *New York Herald Tribune*, August 21, 1927.

9. "Oh, for a Little While Be Kind," *Color*.

10. "Brown Boy to Brown Girl," *Color*.

11. "Pagan Prayer," *Color*.

12. "Oh, for a Little While Be Kind."

13. Cullen, *Crisis*, 31 (March 1926).

14. "Cullen," *Chicago Bee*, December 24, 1927.

15. Cullen, "The Dark Tower," *Opportunity: A Journal of Negro Life*, 5 (June 1927), 80.

16. Ibid., 4 (December 1926), 388.

17. Interview with Lester Walton, *The World*, May 15, 1927.

18. Cullen, "The Dark Tower," *Opportunity*, 5 (June 1927), 181.

19. Ibid. (July 1927), 210.

20. Cullen, ed., *Caroling Dusk* (New York, 1927), p. 179.

21. Cullen, "To Certain Critics," *The Black Christ* (New York, 1929).

22. "Countee Cullen on Miscegenation," *Crisis*, 36 (November 1929), 373.

23. Cullen, "The Dark Tower," 5 (September 1927), 272.

24. Cullen, "Poet on Poet," *Opportunity*, 4 (1926), 73.

25. Interview by Winifred Rothermel, *St. Louis Argus*, February 3, 1928.

26. Cullen, "The Dark Tower," 5 (July 1927), 210.

27. Ibid., 6 (March 1928), 90.

28. Cullen, "The Black Christ," *The Black Christ and Other Poems* (New York, 1929), p. 99.

29. "Surrounded by His Books Countee Cullen Is Happy," p. 6.

30. Cullen, "The Dark Tower," 6 (March 1928), 90.

31. Cullen probably borrowed the idea from Mark Twain's *Huckleberry Finn*. The pretended conversion is one of the Dauphin's favorite methods of fleecing people.

32. Cullen, *One Way to Heaven* (New York, 1932), p. 167.

33. Augustus T. Murray, *Four Plays of Euripides* (Stanford, California, 1931), pp. 111–200.

3 – Zora Neale Hurston

1. Her father was a carpenter and minister, her mother a seamstress. Although her father served three times as mayor of Eatonville, the post offered prominence rather than financial benefit.

2. Zora was the seventh of eight children: five boys, three girls.

3. Although Miss Hurston implied in her autobiography (1942) that she began to work for Miss Hurst before she

graduated from Barnard in 1928, Miss Hurst later asserted that the relationship did not begin until after graduation. Perhaps the issue is not significant; Miss Hurst's memory may have betrayed her about an incident which occurred more than thirty years earlier. Nevertheless, it seems characteristic for Zora Neale Hurston to have claimed distinction to which she was not fully entitled. For instance, in biographical items which she furnished interviewers, Miss Hurston spoke of her work at North Carolina College so ambiguously as to imply a prolonged career as a teacher of drama. In reality, she remained only nine months as a director of dramatics; teachers at the college during that year do not remember that she produced any plays. In another instance, referring to her membership in the American Folklore Society, the American Ethnological Society, and the American Anthropological Society, she implied falsely that these are honorary societies which one may join only if his professional distinction earns him an invitation.

4. Subsequently she received a Rosenwald Fellowship in 1935 and Guggenheim Fellowships in 1936 and 1938.

5. Both in private conversations and in print the sometimes garrulous Zora Neale Hurston was reticent about her marriage. In *Dust Tracks*, she refused even to name her former husband. The marriage was brief. In April 1939 she was still unmarried when Laura Turner and Mamie Knight transported her by automobile from their home in Cincinnati, Ohio, to a speaking engagement at Bennett College in Greensboro, North Carolina. On September 5 of the same year, she wrote to Mamie Knight explaining that, during the iterim, she had married, had immediately felt that she was trapped, and was seeking a divorce.

6. Lewis Garnett of the *New York Herald Tribune* placed her "in the front rank, not only of Negro writers" but of all American writers. Other reviewers praised her for "uncommon gifts as a novelist," "excellent reporting" (in *Mules and Men*), "vivid style," and "good ear for dialect." Margaret Wallace (*New York Times Book Review*, May 6, 1934) described *Jonah's Gourd Vine* as "the most vital and original novel about the American Negro that had yet been written

by a member of the Negro race." Percy Hutchinson (*New York Times*, November 19, 1939) extolled *Moses, Man of the Mountain* as a narrative of great power and "an exceptionally fine piece of work." Theodore Pratt (*Negro Digest*, February 1962) described her as the only "first-class native-born Florida author who has written . . . about the state."

7. Published in 1942, *Dust Tracks* won the Anisfield Wolf Award for its contribution to improving race relations.

8. Fannie Hurst, "Zora Hurston: A Personality Sketch," *Yale University Library Gazette*, 35 (1961), 18.

9. Ibid., p. 19.

10. Ibid., p. 18.

11. A favorite trick of the actors was to whisper messages for the teen-aged Zora to repeat to the actresses. Sometimes the actresses were offended by the messages; more often they were amused. But the teen-aged Zora "innocently" continued to deliver the messages which she did not comprehend. If she had been ten years old rather than seventeen, her pose of naïveté might be credible.

12. Arna Bontemps, review of *Dust Tracks on a Road*, *Books*, November 22, 1942, p. 3.

13. Langston Hughes, "Harlem Literati in the Twenties," *Saturday Review of Literature*, 22 (June 22, 1940), p. 14. Reprinted in *The Big Sea* (New York, 1940), p. 239.

14. Hurst, "Zora Hurston," p. 17.

15. Miss Hurst reported that she once responded to Zora's request that she speak to Zora's anthropology class at Columbia. When Miss Hurst reached the appointed place, however, she learned that Columbia University classes were suspended for Easter vacation.

16. In fairness to Zora Neale Hurston, one must admit that the charm was not lost on blacks. Zora Neale Hurston accomplished feats that are possible only if one possesses magnetism, drive, and complete freedom from inhibition. Langston Hughes reported that she was the only person he knew who could stop a stranger on the streets of Harlem and measure his head for an anthropological survey. Zora Neale Hurston once mailed ten dollars to a friend from whom she had borrowed five. Five dollars of the ten, Miss

Hurston wrote, were to repay the loan, and the other five were to be given to another hospitable friend. Near the end of the letter, Zora Neale Hurston requested her friend also to purchase and send her material which would cost five dollars. The friend dutifully performed both errands and casually attributed the discrepancies to Zora Neale Hurston's habitual confusion about money.

17. In *Tomorrow* (February 1943) Harold Peece described *Dust Tracks* as "the tragedy of a gifted sensitive mind, eaten up by an egocentrism fed on the patronizing admiration of the dominant white world."

18. Hurston, *Dust Tracks on a Road* (Philadelphia, 1942), pp. 293–94.

19. Bontemps, review of *Dust Tracks*, p. 3.

20. Hurston, "I Saw Negro Votes Peddled," *The American Legion Magazine*, November 1950, pp. 12–13, 54–57, 59–60.

21. Perhaps history will prove Zora Neale Hurston wiser than she once seemed to Afro-Americans who optimistically looked only at the advantages of integration. Certainly her fears of the deleterious effects of the influx of white teachers in black schools seem justified in light of recent allegations of the mass firings of black teachers and the demotions of black principals as integration creeps across the South. Although it is to be expected that consolidation of schools might eliminate a few teaching positions, it is alleged that black teachers and principals are the only ones who are being dismissed and that the dismissals are based on race rather than on lack of professional qualifications.

22. Hurston, "A Negro Voter Sizes Up Taft," *The Saturday Evening Post*, December 8, 1951, pp. 29, 150–52.

23. One must use the word "seem," for Zora Neale Hurston's talent or detached point of view enabled her to narrate a horror tale so smoothly that a casual reader may fail to perceive the extent of the horror. In "Sweat," for example, a man weary of his wife attempts to murder her by placing a rattlesnake in her laundry basket. The wife discovers the snake in time to flee safely from the house. In the morning, she waits and watches calmly as her husband, stupefied from

drink, stumbles into the darkened house. She listens to her husband's terrified discovery of the sound of the snake, his frantic search, his screams of awareness that he has been bitten, his desperate battle to kill the snake, and his calls to her for assistance. After waiting until the morning sun has begun to warm the sky, she approaches sufficiently close that her dying husband can see her and know that she has let him die in the trap he set. Then, impelled by a momentary surge of pity, she goes to another part of the yard to wait until he has died.

Like Richard Wright, Zora Neale Hurston understood the violent emotions defining the intrafamilial love-hate relationships of Southern blacks, and she described the disastrous consequences of these emotions. Nevertheless, a reader is less deeply aroused by her descriptions than by the detailed horsors in the works of Richard Wright and Frank Yerby. In her early stories, such as "Sweat," Miss Hurston failed to compel the reader to identify with the characters and to experience their emotions vicariously; consequently, the reader, like the omniscient narrator, maintains a godlike detachment. In her novels, she weighted the family quarrels so heavily with metaphors that the reader, focused on the language, fails to respond fully to the situation.

24. Hurston, *Jonah's Gourd Vine* (Philadelphia, 1934), p. 25.

25. Ibid., p. 9.

26. Ibid., p. 58.

27. Ibid., p. 110.

28. Ibid., p. 113.

29. Ibid., p. 85.

30. Ibid., pp. 156–57.

31. Hurston, *Moses, Man of the Mountain* (Philadelphia, 1939), p. 251.

32. Hurston, *Seraph on the Suwanee* (New York, 1948), p. 154.

33. James Weldon Johnson, *Along This Way* (New York, 1933), pp. 345–46.

34. Ibid., pp. 348–49.

35. Ibid., pp. 359–60.

36. Hurston, *Tell My Horse* (New York, 1938), pp. 100–105.

37. Ibid., p. 93.

38. Johnson, *Along This Way*, pp. 349–50.

39. Hurston, *Tell My Horse*, p. 103.

40. Some puzzled readers have speculated that Miss Hurston took a job as a maid to gather material for a novel. The one which she was preparing at her death, however, concerned Herod the Great. Work was ended by a stroke in 1959.

Works on Black Authors

The American Negro Writer and His Roots. New York: American Society of African Culture, 1960.

Barton, Rebecca C. *Race Consciousness and the American Negro: A Study of the Correlation between the Group Experience and the Fiction of 1900–1930.* Copenhagen: Arnold Busck, 1934.

Bone, Robert A. *The Negro Novel in America.* New Haven: Yale University Press, 1958; rev. ed., 1965.

Brawley, Benjamin. *Early Negro American Writers; Selections with Bibliographical and Critical Introduction.* Chapel Hill, N.C.: University of North Carolina Press, 1935.

————. *The Negro Genius.* New York: Dodd, Mead, 1937.

Brown, Sterling A., et al. *The Negro Caravan.* New York: Dryden, 1941.

————. *The Negro in American Fiction.* Washington, D.C.: Associates in Negro Folk Education, 1937.

————. *Negro Poetry and Drama.* Washington, D.C.: Associates in Negro Folk Education, 1937.

————. *Outline for the Study of the Poetry of American Negroes.* New York: Harcourt, Brace, 1931. (To be used with *The Book of American Negro Poetry.*)

Butcher, Margaret. *The Negro in American Culture.* New York: Knopf, 1956. (Based on materials compiled by Alain Locke.)

Embree, Edwin R. *Thirteen Against the Odds.* New York: Viking, 1945.

Ford, Nick A. *The Contemporary Negro Novel: A Study in Race Relations.* Boston: Meador, 1936.

Franklin, John H. *From Slavery to Freedom.* 2nd ed., rev. New York: Knopf, 1956.

Gloster, Hugh. *Negro Voices in American Fiction.* Chapel Hill, N.C.: University of North Carolina Press, 1948.

Hill, Herbert, ed. *Anger and Beyond: The Negro Writer in the United States.* New York: Harper and Row, 1966.

Hughes, Carl. *The Negro Novelist.* New York: Citadel, 1953.

Hughes, Langston. *The Big Sea.* New York: Knopf, 1940.

Johnson, James W. *Along This Way.* New York: Viking, 1933.

——. *Black Manhattan.* New York: Knopf, 1930.

——, ed. *The Book of American Negro Poetry.* New York: Harcourt, Brace, 1922, 1931.

Jones, LeRoi. *Blues People.* New York: Morrow, 1963.

Locke, Alain, ed. *Four Negro Poets.* New York: Simon and Schuster, 1927. (Works of Claude McKay, Countee Cullen, Jean Toomer, and Langston Hughes.)

——. *The New Negro: An Interpretation.* New York: Albert and Charles Boni, 1925. Especially "The Negro in American Literature" by William S. Braithwaite.

Loften, Mitchell. *Black Drama.* New York: Hawthorn, 1967.

Loggins, Vernon. *The Negro Author: His Development in America to 1900.* New York: Columbia University Press, 1931.

Miller, Elizabeth. *The Negro in America.* Cambridge, Mass.: Harvard University Press, 1966.

Phylon, II (4th Quarter, 1950). Entire issue devoted to articles about black writers.

Porter, Dorothy B. *North American Negro Poets: A Bibliographical Checklist of Their Writings, 1760–1944.* Hattiesburg, Miss.: Book Farm, 1945; rpt. Philadelphia: B. Franklin, 1963.

Redding, J. Saunders. *To Make a Poet Black.* Chapel Hill, N.C.: University of North Carolina Press, 1939.

Turner, Darwin T. *Afro-American Writers.* (A Goldentree Bibliography.) New York: Appleton-Century-Crofts, 1970.

Wagner, Jean. *Les poètes nègres des États-Unis: Le sentiment racial et religeux dans la poésie de P. L. Dunbar à L. Hughes.* Paris: Librairie Istra, 1963.

Whiteman, Maxwell. *A Century of Fiction by American Negroes,* 1853–1952. Philadelphia: Maurice Jacobs, Inc., 1952.

Jean Toomer

BOOKS

Cane. New York: Boni and Liveright, 1923; rpt. New York: University Place Press, 1967; New York: Harper and Row, 1969.

Essentials. Privately printed. Chicago: H. Dupee, 1931.

STORIES (not included in *Cane*)

"Easter." *The Little Review,* 11 (1926), 3–7.

"Mr. Costyve Duditch." *Dial,* 85 (December 1928), 460–76.

"Of a Certain November." *Dubuque Dial,* November 1, 1935.

"Winter on Earth." *Second American Caravan: A Yearbook of American Literature.* Ed. Kreymborg, Mumford, and Rosenfeld. New York: Macaulay, 1928.

"York Beach." *New American Caravan.* Ed. Kreymborg, Mumford, and Rosenfeld. New York: Macaulay, 1929.

POEMS (not included in *Cane*)

"Banking Coal." *Crisis,* 24 (1922), 65.

"The Blue Meridian." *The New Caravan.* Ed. Kreymborg et al. New York: Macaulay, 1936.

"Brown River, Smile" (first 125 lines of "The Blue Meridian"). *The Adelphi,* 2 (September 1931). Also published in *Pagany,* 3 (Winter 1932), 29–33.

"Five Vignettes," "The Lost Dancer," "At Sea," and the concluding lines of "The Blue Meridian." *Black American Literature: Poetry.* Ed. Darwin T. Turner. Columbus, Ohio: Charles Merrill, 1969.

"Reflections." *Dial,* 86 (1929), 314.

"See the Heart." *Friend's Intelligencer,* 104 (August 9, 1947), 423.

"White Arrow." *Dial,* 86 (July 1929), 596.

PLAYS

"Balo." *Plays of Negro Life*. Ed. Alain Locke and Gregory Montgomery. New York: Harper and Brothers, 1927.

DIALOGUES

"Good and Bad Artists." *The New Mexico Sentinel*, 1937.
"Make Good." *The New Mexico Sentinel*, 1937.
"Socratic Dialogue." *The New Mexico Sentinel*, 1941.

ARTICLES

"A New Force for Co-operation." *The Adelphi* (1934).
"The South in Literature." *The Call* (1923).

AUTOBIOGRAPHIES

"Chapters from *Earth Being*." *The Black Scholar*, 2 (January 1971), 3–14.
A Fiction and Some Facts. Privately published [1931].

UNPUBLISHED NOVELS, Toomer Collection, Fisk University

"Caromb." [1932]
"The Gallonwerps." [1927]; revised 1933.
"Transatlantic." [1929]; revised as "Eight Day World." [1933]; revised 1934.

UNPUBLISHED PLAYS, Toomer Collection

"A Drama of the Southwest" (incomplete). [1926]
"The Gallonwerps." 1927.
"Natalie Mann." [1921]
"The Sacred Factory." 1927.

UNPUBLISHED PHILOSOPHICAL WORKS, Toomer Collection

"From Exile into Being." [1940]; revised as "The Second River" [1941].
"The Individual in America." 1929.
"Istil." [1929]; revised as "York Beach."

"Living is Developing." Undated.
"Portage Potential." [1932]
"Remember and Return." [1931]
"Talks with Peter." [1937]
"Values and Fictions." 1927.

UNPUBLISHED POETRY, Toomer Collection

"Blue Meridian and Other Poems." [1933]
"Bride of Air." [1931]

UNPUBLISHED STORIES, Toomer Collection

"Drackman." [1928]
"Love on a Train." [1928]
"Lump." [1928]
"Mr. Limph Krok's Famous 'L' Ride." [1930]
"Two Professors." [1930]
"Withered Skin of Berries." [1930]

UNPUBLISHED AUTOBIOGRAPHIES, Toomer Collection

See the discussion of the autobiographies in footnote 13, chapter 1.
"Autobiography." [1936]
"Earth Being." [1930]
"Incredible Journey." [1945]
"Outline of an Autobiography." [1946]

WORKS ABOUT TOOMER

Bontemps, Arna. The Harlem Renaissance." *Saturday Review*, 30 (March 22, 1947), 12–13, 44.
———. "The Negro Renaissance: Jean Toomer and the Harlem of the 1920's." *Anger and Beyond: The Negro Writer in the United States*. New York: Harper and Row, 1966, pp. 20–36.
Dillard, Mabel. "Jean Toomer: Herald of the Negro Renaissance." Ph.D. diss. Ohio University, 1967.
DuBois, W. E. B. and Alain Locke. "The Younger Literary Movement." *Crisis*, 27 (1924), 161–63.

Fullinwider, S. P. "Jean Toomer, Lost Generation, or Negro Renaissance?" *Phylon*, 27 (1966), 396–403.

Gloster, Hugh M. *Negro Voices in American Fiction*. Chapel Hill, N.C.: University of North Carolina Press, 1948.

Gregory, Montgomery. Review of *Cane*. *Opportunity*, 1 (1923), 374–75.

Holmes, Eugene. "Jean Toomer, Apostle of Beauty." *Opportunity*, 3 (1925), 252–54, 260.

Littell, Robert. Review of *Cane*. *New Republic*, 37 (1923), 126.

Locke, Alain. *Four Negro Poets*. New York: Simon and Schuster, 1927.

———. "From *Native Son* to *Invisible Man*: A Review of the Literature for 1952." *Phylon*, 14 (1953), 34–44.

Munson, Gorham. "Correspondence." *New York Times*, February 16, 1969, 7:54.

———. "The Significance of Jean Toomer." *Opportunity*, 3 (1925), 262–63.

Rosenfeld, Paul. "Jean Toomer." *Men Seen*. New York: Dial, 1925, pp. 227–36.

Turner, Darwin T. "And Another Passing." *Negro American Literature Forum*, Fall 1967, pp. 3–4.

———. "Jean Toomer's *Cane*." *Negro Digest*, 18 (January 1969), 54–61.

———. "The Failure of a Playwright." *College Language Association Journal*, 10 (1966), 308–18.

Countee Cullen

BOOKS

The Ballad of the Brown Girl. New York: Harper and Brothers, 1927.

The Black Christ and Other Poems. New York: Harper and Brothers, 1929.

Caroling Dusk (Ed.). New York: Harper and Brothers, 1927.

Color. New York: Harper and Brothers, 1925.

Copper Sun. New York: Harper and Brothers, 1927.

One Way to Heaven. New York: Harper and Brothers, 1932.

The Lost Zoo. New York: Harper and Brothers, 1940.

The Medea and Some Poems. New York: Harper and Brothers, 1935.

My Lives and How I Lost Them. New York: Harper and Brothers, 1942.

On These I Stand. New York: Harper and Brothers, 1947.

PLAYS

With Arna Bontemps. "St. Louis Woman." Unpublished; manuscript is in the Schomburg Collection of the New York City Public Library.

With Owen Dodson. "The Third Fourth of July." *Theatre Arts,* 30 (August 1946), 488–93.

ARTICLES (selected)

"Poet on a Poet." *Opportunity: A Journal of Negro Life,* 4 (February 1926), 73–74.

"The Dark Tower" (a monthly column). *Opportunity: A Journal of Negro Life,* 4 (December 1926), 388–90; 5 (January 1927), 24–25; (February 1927), 53–54; (March, 1927), 86–87; (April 1927), 118–19; (May 1927), 149–50; (June 1927), 180–81; (July 1927), 210–11; (August 1927), 240–41; (September 1927), 272–73; (November 1927), 336–37; (December 1927), 373–74; 6 (January 1928), 20–21; (February 1928), 52–53; (March 1928), 90; (April 1928), 120; (May 1928), 146–47; (June 1928), 178–79; (July 1928), 210; (September 1928), 271–73.

"Countee Cullen to His Friends." *Crisis,* 36 (April 1929), 119.

"Countee Cullen on French Courtesy." *Crisis,* 36 (June 1929), 193.

"Countee Cullen in England." *Crisis,* 36 (August 1929), 270, 283.

"Countee Cullen on Miscegenation." *Crisis,* 36 (November 1929), 373.

WORKS ABOUT CULLEN

Bontemps, Arna. "Countee Cullen, American Poet." *The People's Voice,* January 26, 1946, pp. 52–53.

———. "The Harlem Renaissance." *Saturday Review*, 30 (March 22, 1947), 12–13, 44.

———. "The James Weldon Johnson Memorial Collection of Negro Arts and Letters." *Yale University Library Gazette*, 18 (October 1943), 19–26.

Bronz, Stephen A. *Roots of Racial Consciousness; the 1920's: Three Harlem Renaissance Authors.* New York: Libra, 1964.

Davis, Arthur. "The Alien and Exile Theme in Countee Cullen's Racial Poems." *Phylon*, 14 (1953), 390–400.

Dodson, Owen. "Countee Cullen (1903–1946)." *Phylon*, 7 (1946), 19–21.

Ferguson, Blanche E. *Countee Cullen and the Negro Renaissance.* New York: Dodd, Mead, 1966.

Gloster, Hugh M. *Negro Voices in American Fiction.* Chapel Hill, N.C.: Univ. of North Carolina Press, 1948.

Hughes, Langston. "The Negro Artist and the Racial Mountain." *Nation*, 122 (1926), 692–94.

Johnson, Charles, ed. "Countee Cullen." *Source Materials for Patterns of Negro Segregation.* Volume 8. Schomburg Collection, New York City Public Library.

Lash, John S. "The Anthologist and the Negro Author." *Phylon*, 8 (1947), 68–76.

Locke, Alain. *Four Negro Poets.* New York: Simon and Schuster, 1927.

Perry, Margaret. *A Bio-Bibliography of Countee P. Cullen.* Westport, Conn.: Greenwood, 1971.

Reimherr, Beulah. "Countee Cullen: A Biographical and Critical Study." M.A. thesis, University of Maryland, 1960.

———. "Race Consciousness in Countee Cullen's Poetry." *Susquehanna University Studies*, 7, No. 2 (1963), 65–82.

Robb, Izetta W. "From the Darker Side." *Opportunity*, 4 (1926), 381–82.

Smith, Robert. "The Poetry of Countee Cullen." *Phylon*, 11 (1950), 216–21.

Webster, Harvey. "A Difficult Career." *Poetry*, 70 (1947), 222–25.

Whithorne, Emerson. *The Grim Troubadour*. New York: Fisher, 1927.

Woodruff, Bertram. "The Poetic Philosophy of Countee Cullen." *Phylon*, 1 (1940), 213–23.

Zora Neale Hurston

BOOKS

Dust Tracks on a Road. Philadelphia: J. B. Lippincott, 1942.

Jonah's Gourd Vine. Philadelphia: J. B. Lippincott, 1934.

Moses, Man of the Mountain. Philadelphia: J. B. Lippincott, 1939.

Mules and Men. Philadelphia: J. B. Lippincott, 1935; rpt. New York: Collier, 1970.

Seraph on the Suwanee. New York: Charles Scribner's Sons, 1948.

Tell My Horse. Philadelphia: J. B. Lippincott, 1938.

Their Eyes Were Watching God. Philadelphia: J. B. Lippincott, 1937.

ARTICLES

"I Saw Negro Votes Peddled." *American Legion Magazine*, November 1950, pp. 12–13, 45–57, 59–60.

"A Negro Voter Sizes Up Taft." *The Saturday Evening Post*, 224 (December 8, 1951), 29, 150–152.

"What White Publishers Won't Print." *Negro Digest*, 5 (April 1947), 85–89.

STORIES

"Drenched in Light." *Opportunity*, 2 (December 1924), 371–74.

"The Gilded Six Bits." *Story in America*. Ed. Whit Burnett and Martha Foley. New York: Vanguard, 1934, pp. 73–84.

"John Redding Goes to Sea." *Opportunity*, 4 (January 1926), 16–21.

"Spunk." *Opportunity*, 3 (May 1925), 171–73.

"Sweat." *Black American Literature: Essays, Poetry, Fiction, Drama*. Ed. Darwin T. Turner. Columbus, Ohio: Merrill, 1970, pp. 339–50. Originally published in *Fire*, 1 (December 1926).

PLAYS

"The First One, a Play." *Ebony and Topaz, a Collectanea*. Ed. Charles S. Johnson. New York: National Urban League, 1927.

UNPUBLISHED WORKS

"Book of Harlem."

"The Chick with One Hen."

"The Emperor Effaces Himself in Harlem Language."

"Mulebone: A Comedy of Negro Life in Three Acts" by Langston Hughes and Zora Neale Hurston, New York, 1931.

"Polk County, A Comedy of Negro Life on a Sawmill Camp."

WORKS ABOUT HURSTON

Byrd, James W. "Zora Neale Hurston: A Novel Folklorist." *Tennessee Folklore Society Bulletin*, 21 (1955), 37–41.

Hughes, Langston. "Black Renaissance." *The Big Sea*. New York: Knopf, 1940.

Hurst, Fannie. "Zora Hurston: A Personality Sketch." *Yale University Library Gazette*, 35 (1961), 17–22.

Jackson, Blyden. "Some Negroes in the Land of Goshen." *Tennessee Folklore Society Bulletin*, 19 (1953), 103–07.

Pratt, Theodore. "A Memoir: Zora Neale Hurston, Florida's First Distinguished Author." *Negro Digest*, February 1962, pp. 52–56.

Turner, Darwin T. "The Negro Novelist and the South." *Southern Humanities Review*, 1 (1967), 21–29.

Index

Acker, Merrall, Conduit Company, 9
Afro-Americans: literary creativity, xvi, 2, 34; stereotypes of, xvii, 67, 87
Anderson, Sherwood: praise of Toomer, 2, 4, 127n59; on Toomer's style, 3; literary influence on Toomer, 11, 19, 124n23, 126n42

Baldwin, James, xx
Ballad of the Brown Girl, The. See Cullen, Countee
Black Christ, The. See Cullen Countee
Boas, Franz, 90, 92
Bone, Robert: on *Cane*, 5, 6; on Hurston, 101, 113
Boni and Liveright, Inc.: contract for *Cane*, 14; Toomer's rejection of identification as Negro, 32; acceptance of *Cane*, 126n42. *See also* Liveright, Horace
Bontemps, Arna: as writer, xix; on Toomer, 5; on Hurston, 92, 95
Braithwaite, William Stanley, 2
Brawley, Benjamin, xviii, 4
Bronz, Stephen: on Cullen, 60
Brooks, Gwendolyn, xx, xxi

Broom, 1, 14
Brown, William Wells, xv, 116
Burke, Kenneth, 33, 44
Bynner, Witter: on Cullen, 64; poetry contests, 64, 65

Cane: critical reactions, 2; significance, 3–5; analysis, 14–30; structure, 14, 124–25n-23; swan song, 30; influences on, 126n42
Caroling Dusk, 63
Chesnutt, Charles W., xvi, 2, 117
Christopher Cat, 85–87 passim
Color. See Cullen, Countee
Content, Marjorie. *See* Toomer, Marjorie Content
Copper Sun, 63, 73
Crane, Hart, 33
Cullen Countee: literary reputation, xix, xxi–xxii, 60, 64, 66, 67, 69, 70, 72–74 passim, 88; on Africa, 61, 65, 67, 68, 84; on love, 61, 68, 74, 84; on poetry, 61, 71, 73; desire for black god, 61, 68, 75–77; education, 62; life, 62–63; parents, 62; literary prizes, 62–65 passim; strengths as poet, 63–64, 68,